CULTURE SHOCK!

A Survival Guide to Customs and Etiquette

BALI

Paul Winslow

T0294196

Marshall Cavendish
Editions

ABOUT THE SERIES

Culture shock is a state of disorientation that can come over
...into unknown surroundings, away
...CultureShock! is a series of trusted
...has, for decades, been helping
...isitors to cushion the impact of
...move to a new country.
...ave lived in the country and
...hemselves, the authors share
...or anyone to cope with these
...e effectively. The guides are
...o read and covers a range of
...enough advice, hints and tips
...possible again.
...he same manner. It begins
...itors will have of that city or
...ne must first understand the
...ho they are, the values and
...eir customs and etiquette.
...e book.
...cts—how to settle in with
...aders through how to find
...d telecommunications up
...ool and keep in the pink of
...entials are out of the way,
...e of the culture and travel
...e language of the country
...siness side of things.
...ion are offered before
...tiquette. Useful words
...rce guide and list of
...ed for easy reference.

ıl (Asia) Private Limited

ıs
tional
}

s Road, Tarrytown NY 10591-9001, USA •
td. 253 Asoke, 12th Flr, Sukhumvit 21 Road,
nd • Marshall Cavendish (Malaysia) Sdn Bhd,
' Park, Batu Tiga, 40000 Shah Alam, Selangor

shing Limited

'ublication Data

is and etiquette / Paul Winslow

i, [2016]
8-2 (paperback)
iia)--Social life and customs. | Etiquette--
nesian.

45, 46, 49, 59, 66, 96: James Dauman;
ards; 81: Mark Carolan

ACKNOWLEDGMENTS

Thanks to Ben for the referral, to Rachel for her faith
and to She-reen for all her help and encouragement.
More thanks to KT, Ned, Weiley, Joar, Nicole, Gary,
Adam and James for their contributions. A nod to
Mark for the photos he took when he was actually
on the island. To Ned for inspiring the dream and to
Rae—if you hadn't encouraged me to chase the dream
I wouldn't be living it now. And to the Bali Lost Boys—
the football and social life is such a big part of my Bali
existence even if you never do what I say.

CONTENTS

Introduction viii

Map of Bali xi

Chapter 1
First Impressions 1

Welcome to Paradise 2

What the Hell Am I Doing
Here?—A Blog Post 6

Don't Judge a Book
By Its Cover 10

Chapter 2
Geography and History 15

A Drop in the Ocean 16

High and Mighty 18

Fields of Dreams 20

Going Wild 25

Blood, Sweat and Tears 28

Nosy Neighbours 29

Going Dutch 31

War Stories 34

Chapter 3
The People of Bali 41

Standing on Ceremony 42

Chapter 4
Fitting Into Society 57

Rubbing Along Nicely 58

Visitng a Balinese 64

Chapter 5
Diving In To Bali Life 71

Being Legal—Visas 73

A Load of Bankers 77

Taxing Matters 81

Completely Up Front 82

Lease of Faith 89

Shopping Around 91

Driving Force 94

Class Act 103

A Healthy Attitude 105

Chapter 6
Selemat Makan 109

Going Local 111

Do It Yourself 114

Going Upmarket 119

Lazy Sundays 125

Keeping It Real 126

Chapter 7
Exploring Paradise 131

Treasure Island 132

Riding the Waves 138

Namaste 141

Going Under 142

Adrenaline Rush 144

...And Relax 145

In the Swing 147

A Walk In the Park   149

Holy Ground   150

Dancing Shoes   154

More to See   157

Good Sport   160

A Drop In the Ocean   162

Let's Celebrate   162

Chapter 8
How Do You Say...?   164

Where Can I Learn?   167

A Word to the Wise   169

It's Not Just What You Say,
It's How You Say It   170

Numbers Game   172

Speak Like A Local   173

Chapter 9
Working and
Running a Business   174

Maybe on Tuesday   175

Voluntary Service   183

Chapter 10
Fast Facts   184

Culture Quiz   188

Do's and Don'ts   192

Glossary   194

Resource Guide   198

Further Reading   206

About the Author   209

Index   210

INTRODUCTION

Bali. A word with magical connotations. While there is a boring dictionary definition, it's impossible to quantify exactly because Bali means different things to different people. It's a highly personal place.

For some it is synonymous with surfing. For others it inspires visions of palm trees and beaches. Some picture rolling ricefields and blue skies stretching to the horizon. And others may link it inextricably with one section of the 2006 novel *Eat, Pray, Love* or its 2010 film adaptation. It has magical connotations that can appeal beyond its borders, even to those who have never been fortunate enough to sample its myriad attractions.

Bali has a negative side too. Its international appeal has been tarnished because of the executions of drug dealers, by stories of wild nightlife and drunken excess and still, over a decade on, the distant hangover of two terrorist bombings can be felt.

As with any place in the world, good mixes with bad. This is a paradise with blemishes. But that's planet earth— nowhere's perfect.

Before coming to live in Bali I had been a one-time visitor with no real desire to return. It wasn't that I disliked it, but I'd studiously avoided the touristy areas and had no real desire to visit them. Now I happily live in one of the island's biggest.

Explaining the charm of Bali for tourists is easy. The sun, sand, sea, surf and culture at a price that's right are hugely attractive wherever you call home. If you happen to be from Australia then there's a very practical element to it as well— it's pretty much the first stepping stone on your way to the rest of the world and when you combine that with the other attractions it's easy to see why it's such a perennial favourite. But for those who choose to spend longer here there's a subtle difference.

There's a saying amongst those people who have lived in Asia for a long time that nobody really moves to the region intentionally, they just arrive and never leave. But more often than not to live in Asia means living in a big city (Singapore, Hong Kong, Manila, Jakarta to name a few) or out in the middle of nowhere. Bali offers the best of both worlds. It has the seductive combination of people, culture, streetfood, climate etc—and it also has the infrastructure—roads, community, Internet, electricity, restaurants, schools etc.

Bali is a place that takes the best of everything and mixes it into a pot pourri of all that's good with Asia, with the comforts decadent westerners desire, without living in a big, horrible, nasty city.

But Bali's true allure is almost indescribable—all the aforementioned things have a place but it's more than that; there's something about it that inspires passion and desire, a certain something you can never put your finger on.

And that explains why it's mighty difficult to leave, and probably explains why I'm still here writing this book.

Stepping up: Bali is the land of a thousand temples—
if you're being really conservative with your counting!

MAP OF BALI

CHAPTER 1

FIRST IMPRESSIONS

Bali Ha'i will whisper In the wind of the sea:
❝Here I am your special island! Come to me,
come to me❞

– Bali Ha'i, South Pacific

WELCOME TO PARADISE

"Maybe you should spend the first six months of your travels in Bali."

It sounds such an innocuous sentence when I cut and paste it from the email now. But it was the sentence that changed my life, because "the first six months" have become two years, while the "travels" remain on hold and will do for some time to come.

Not that this is entirely surprising. In 2009 I'd left the UK 'for a year' and had yet to make my way back for anything more than a fleeting visit so this is standard behaviour. But I really didn't think Bali would suck me in the way it did.

The words had been typed in an email by my good friend Ned, an old colleague who had coincidentally left the UK around the same time as I did. But while my life diversion had taken me to Australia, his ship had dropped anchor in Bali. Now he was suggesting that our paths realign, not just in terms of where we resided but that of our publisher-editor relationship. He was launching a magazine; I edit magazines for a living (and write books, it seems). I had itchy feet;

Star attraction: Bintang is ubiquitous in Bali—I've consumed one or two in my time here.

he had his feet in flip-flops. I was paying US$ 8 for a beer and he was paying less than US$ 2. It didn't take long to come to the conclusion that this was an opportunity worth serious consideration.

But what did I know of Bali? I had spent a small amount of time there on my aforementioned world tour. After eleven months of getting off the beaten track in Africa and Asia, my travel companion and I had assumed an air of backpacker snobbery and harboured no desire to hang around with 'holidaymakers' or 'tourists'. Although Bali was on our route, we got out of Dodge immediately upon landing, avoiding the major tourist areas as if our very ethos of life would be spoilt by our presence there.

And that's because the first impressions of a place like Bali come way before you touch down on the tarmac of the airport. Back in 2010 the word 'Bali' had connotations of a beautiful island tainted with a reputation of insalubrious tourism, of downmarket rowdiness. Like so many places with such a reputation there is a truth to it, but it is only one small part of the bigger truth. But I wasn't really too interested in working all that out on my first short visit so didn't experience the Bali that millions of tourists do each year. And nothing I learned while living in Melbourne for over three years did anything to convince me that I had missed anything. Phrases such as: "it's like Australia's Magaluf or Tenerife" were enough to put me off completely.

You may, then, be forgiven for wondering why on earth I would ever consider throwing in my lot and moving to such a place. But there's a huge difference between going on holiday somewhere and living there and I figured that to live in such a place would mean opening up a whole new side of it. The weather, standard of living, lifestyle, new adventure—added to the fact our new magazine project would involve reviewing a litany of high-class establishments—all factored in to make it something of a no-brainer experiment. Supported by my partner, the decision was made. Bali here we come.

In the weeks running up to my departure, Australia's Channel 7 began showing a documentary series called *What Really Happens in Bali*. It was truly awful. Drunken idiots falling off scooters and ending up in hospital, footage of the Bali 9 prisoners in Kerobokan prison, inebriated teenagers staggering the streets and laneways, health and safety nightmares and rip-off merchants all combined to paint a hideous picture. Fortunately it was also transparent—it could easily have been called *What Really Happens Anywhere Young People Go On Holiday And Drink Too Much*. At least I hoped so.

I was to be pleasantly surprised. Not only was Bali not like the TV show, it was not like the reputation. Sure, Bali has a less salubrious side, but then so do many places. And the rest more than makes up for it.

On reflection: Rice paddies make for a perennially pretty picture.

None of which I knew on my first day tentatively exploring my new surroundings. When I dredge the depths of my memory for what I may have been thinking then, several things stand out that were probably running through my mind. The simple beauty of rice fields, the inability of the Balinese to construct a pavement that (a) doesn't have holes in it and (b) run smoothly for any more than 15 metres. The ubiquitous small baskets placed on the ground and on temples (more of them later). The lack of any apparent rules of the road. The Balinese people going about their business mingling with the many holidaymakers going about theirs. And the weather… the wonderful weather.

To really write this chapter effectively would require a time machine so I can fully appreciate my state of mind upon my arrival. Fortunately, I do have an ersatz time machine in the form of a blog post written just a few days after my arrival. This was originally intended as my first 'postcard from Bali' to let my friends know about my new adventure but it's now the perfect way to portray my actual first impressions for the purposes of this publication.

After a week of immersing myself in my new life, this was the effect it had on me:

Rice, rice, baby: It feeds people and creates a beautiful backdrop to life in Bali.

WHAT THE HELL AM I DOING HERE? —A BLOG POST

They say a week is a long time in politics. I wouldn't know about that but I do know a week is a long time in Bali when you've just upped sticks and moved here. This time last week I had never seen the studio apartment I am writing this in. I'd never seen the *Essential Bali* office, didn't know my new colleagues and had only intermittently driven mopeds on crazy roads in third world countries. I didn't know my Seminyak from my Legian and I'd certainly never had a daily house cleaner who would take my laundry away and bring it back freshly cleaned a couple of days later.

Now all of those things seem, well, not exactly second nature, but certainly part and parcel of life…

And lo, last Monday Ned did pick me up from Bali airport… We dumped my bags in the studio that had until that day been his home and was now mine. (He had moved somewhere else—I hadn't kicked him out onto the beach). It's a reasonable size room with a decent bed, a shower that boasts both power and hot water, and a lovely outside area with a garden that is shared by another studio. Being down a small laneway it's quite quiet… as long as the dogs aren't barking, the cocks crowing or the kids shouting, but to be fair that's not often. The 'kitchen' facilities leave something to be desired, consisting as they do of a single gas ring linked to a gas bottle, but it's home, temporarily, and I am becoming quite attached to it. My man Noor coming by everyday to make it pristine and run errands for me does nothing to harm that situation.

Ned took me to his local... as we ordered the first of lord knows how many Bintangs to come over the next few months in the warm air, I felt a different kind of home. Moving somewhere isn't the same as travelling—but moving to a place like this is somewhere in the middle.

Waking on my first day, the priority was breakfast so I ambled in the direction of Seminyak. I live just on the other side of the tracks from where the famous suburb begins and after dodging the missing paving slabs and therefore avoiding falling into the running water (water—well that's one word for it) below I strolled past a rice paddy and into Seminyak. I headed for the first half decent place I saw and found it to be Bali Deli—famous among Australian visitors for having about the best coffee in the area. It's worth pointing out that this shows the evolution of Bali in itself. Bali Deli is now a shadow of its former self and the coffee is much better in many other places.

Then it was time for Ned to pick me up on his moped and take me to the office (passing Kerobokan Prison en route—I work about 50 metres away) to meet Ana and Ayu, my Indonesian colleagues who have proved to be great fun already. When it came to lunch, Ned suggested Ana show me somewhere to get a bite. This was funny because she decided that I should drive the moped while she was on the back. It makes practical sense as you don't want the heavy bloke on the back with the light lady on the front. It didn't make such practical sense as I'd only driven one about three times in my life and could barely remember what to do. Somehow we made it to a café and back alive.

By this time I had realised that mopeds are the only way to get around, so Ned got on the phone to hire me one. The traffic in Bali is just nuts—not as nuts as Vietnam, so maybe incessant is a better word. I'm not sure I'll ever get used to it, but what I will get used to is Ned turning round at the end of the working day and suggesting a sunset beer. It was slightly weird heading down to a beach bar where everyone else was on holiday and we'd just finished a day at the office. I think I will get used to that as well.

Emotions were a bit all over the place at this point. I wanted to know my way round, I wanted to know the language, I wanted to not have to drive through all that bloody traffic to get anywhere. No matter how many times you pack it all in and leave home, and I've done it enough now, I think there's always a moment when you think 'what the **** have I done here?' even if in your hearts of hearts you know the answer is 'what I have done here is open the door to a great new adventure and it's going to be bloody amazing.'

Pedalling your wares: If you won't come to the goods, the goods will usually come to you.

This uncertainty was probably exacerbated by my attempts that night to find the Bintang Supermarket, which is not a supermarket full of Bintang but one of the best supermarkets in Seminyak. The building I entered looked as though it hadn't sold any food for years. If you can imagine going to a supermarket in Chernobyl today, left exactly as it was when the accident happened, then you'd get the kind of feel. There was no deli, no fruit, nothing fresher than Prince Phillip. I bought some pasta and dodgy-looking bolognaise sauce, having promised myself I would cook at home that night to get out of eating out all the time as if I was on holiday. If this was the best Seminyak had to offer then what the **** have I done here?

DON'T JUDGE A BOOK BY ITS COVER
Before you get too concerned that Bali doesn't have any supermarkets, it turned out that if I had bothered to walk 20 metres further I would have discovered the one I was

actually seeking. It had these remarkable products such as fruit, vegetables and meat and looked as though the shelves were replenished at least once every millennium. It became crystal clear why the store I originally visited never sold anything because only a complete idiot (i.e. me) would shop there when there was a perfectly good supermarket within throwing distance of the rotten eggs they were probably selling. It does sum up a strange dichotomy here: you can have stores that appear to have stopped ordering in anything new several years ago next to fully stocked modern enterprises. And even then you will be lucky to find everything you need in one shop — even the big hypermarkets don't cover every base. But other than a few things (good chocolate being my personal bugbear) you'll find most things somewhere.

It's funny looking back now how much first impressions are based on practicalities rather than surroundings. When you first arrive in a new place to live, as opposed to holiday, there are certain things you need to sort out and most of them are much more boring than going out to explore the really good bits. And that part about coming here for a reason other than a holiday. Well that can have a huge effect on your first impressions as well. Whether you're here for business or to emigrate, you're doing so in a tourist capital. And that means you'll get treated like a tourist. You will struggle to walk past a spa without being asked if you want a massage, you'll have the same issue walking past pretty much any eating establishment while you'll also get asked if you want transport even when you've brought your own. You might get offered the opportunity to go on a tourist excursion and equally, you might get offered "Xanax? Valium? Viagra?" It only tends to happen on the major tourist thoroughfares but you're certain to explore those in your early days and the temptation to say "No, I live here" can be overwhelming. Eventually it just cascades off you like the proverbial water off a duck's back.

Set your stall out: Street food can be found on nearly every corner.

The reality is that first impressions of anywhere are going to be based not just on that place, but also on your own experiences in life prior to that. The wall of heat that greets you when you walk out of the airport is something that can scramble the brain if it's something you haven't encountered before. Or it may kick-start multiple memories of times spent in similarly tropical climates. The traffic can inspire you or scare you. The uneven pavements are something you literally take in your stride, or they boggle your brain. The badgering of the touts may be something you've encountered and can brush off or they can be off putting.

But I find myself nearing the end of this chapter having missed probably the most important bits. This is a tropical island with palm trees everywhere you look, with beach and surf, with friendly locals, with beautiful scenery and epic mountains. It's the little things that make first impressions, but they are quickly superseded by the big things that leave the lasting ones.

Our visit to Bali was meant to be a temporary one; a four-month pit stop before heading to South America. But we loved it here so much we decided to stay.

We spent a week in a resort in Nusa Dua and it was nice but generic; it could have been any beach resort in Asia. We then headed up to Ubud. The traffic was terrible that day but it gave us time to really study the architecture of the houses along the roads. They seemed all so neat and tidy and all signs of the chaos of family life are hidden away behind walled compounds, where several generations of a family share residence.

It took several weeks to get used to carrying around what seemed like a lot of cash (feeling like a millionaire), and even longer to work out the traffic laws when riding a scooter (I'm still not sure if there are any). Navigating crossroads was interesting… although somehow it always goes smoothly and no one gets road rage (must be all the ceremonies). Little brushes with death, such as slipping on loose gravel or being driven off the road by a lorry or tourist bus are shrugged off as 'one of those things'. All sense of urgency is lost here; there seem to be no such thing as timekeeping. Each house in Ubud has its own well, which means every family enjoys free water, but the locals still choose to bathe and wash their clothes in the streams that run through the town.

We found the Balinese to be welcoming and warm, honest and generous. It took a while to get used to not having to haggle (after living in Thailand for two years we've had a lot of practice) as no one was actually trying to rip us off. I guess our first impressions of Bali are probably biased as Ubud is in its own little essential oil-anointed bubble, where positive energy and healthy living are the daily mantras.

– Weiley Walter, arrived in Bali 2015

My first week was spent being driven round from Kuta up to Petitenget in Seminyak. I didn't really venture further than that for a good few weeks until I got a moped, so my initial time was very limited geographically.

It was a lot more sophisticated than I expected. I was expecting dirt tracks like in some of the archive photos I still use on our Facebook page but the roads are actually pretty good. I certainly didn't expect a three-lane highway on my doorstep. It was almost disappointingly modern.

But then those roads are necessary because of the mayhem of the traffic. I'd spent two months prior to my arrival in India, so it shouldn't have been a shock, but it was. I remember being told in India that as a pedestrian if you walk confidently and wave at vehicles they will usually stop. I tried to use the same theory here and was quickly put right. The roads are lawless and they scared the shit out of me initially.

In all honesty I didn't like it at first. I was stuck in Dhyana Pura / Double Six (major tourist areas) with no desire to rent a moped. For someone arriving fresh today and being thrown into middle of Seminyak, I'd recommend a Jimbaran lunch and a trip to Tanah Lot, if not for the temple, then for the rice fields en route. And do it in the first few days so you realise quickly there is escape from the tourists.

But if the tourists did nothing for me, the locals did. Hindus, Muslims and Christians living side-by-side in harmony amazed me, particularly when you have the highly ritualistic Balinese with their multiple daily offerings and closing streets for their ceremonies, and then the Muslim call to prayer at 5:00 am every morning if you live next to a mosque.

My overriding memory and still lasting impression is of the smiles. Thailand is supposed to be the country of a thousand smiles or something but they're miserable by contrast. I still can't work it out. The Balinese are, or at least seem to be, happier than most. They have an inner peace, one you'd more associate with Buddhism.

– Ned Dean, arrived in Bali 2011

CHAPTER 2

GEOGRAPHY AND HISTORY

Pre-Colonial Bali bore little resemblance to the idyllic vision of later European visitors. Warfare, disease and natural disaster were all commonplace.

– **Robert Pringle,** *A Short History of Bali*

A DROP IN THE OCEAN

The tropical island of Bali lies sandwiched between its immense neighbour Java, just 3.2 km (2 miles) to the west, and Lombok, around 30 km (18.6 miles) to the east. The island is the major landmass in the province of the same name that also includes numerous other smaller islands, including Nusa Lembongan, Nusa Penida and Nusa Ceningan. It stretches around 145 km (90 miles) east to west and 112 km (69.6 miles) north to south and is just one of 17,508 islands that make up the country of Indonesia (depending on whose figures you believe—I go by the CIA World Factbook). It accounts for just 0.3 per cent of the total landmass of the world's fourth most populous country and the island's population of around 4.5 million accounts for less than two per cent of Indonesia's population.

In sheer numbers then, Bali is a fairly insignificant piece of this immense archipelago puzzle. It may be small, but Bali has a cultural and economic significance far outweighing its size, which explains why it is a mecca for both tourists, expats looking for a more laidback way of life and Indonesians looking for the employment created as a result.

Yet its appeal and magical allure distort its relevance. This can be unscientifically measured in a couple of ways. Firstly, if you mention you live here you'll find people going all misty-eyed and jealous even if they have never visited, don't know what it's like or even where it is. And then there's the number of times you'll get asked, "So, erm, is Bali a separate country?" Do a pop quiz of the people around you and I'm convinced 50 per cent of them will think Bali is a nation state.

Its main tourist and population centres are concentrated on the southern end of the island, with a stretch from Kuta through Legian and Seminyak to Canggu on the southwest coast, while on the tiny peninsula that looks as though it is attached to the rest of the island by a thin thread you'll find the huge, luxury tourist resorts in Nusa Dua and beyond. Between them all lays the capital of Denpasar, while the spiritual town of Ubud can be found just a few kilometres north.

All at sea: Boats for all seasons and all reasons at Padang Bai.

So much for the statistics and the basics but they tell little of the actual story. Geography is, according to a very handy source "the description, distribution, and interaction of the diverse physical, biological, and cultural features of the earth's surface". I use that definition here, because when you consider it you begin to understand why Bali is what it is, because when Mother Nature was doling out her goodies, she was very generous to Bali. Very generous indeed.

Close your eyes and imagine your perfect island. Some big volcanic mountains, leading down to stunning plateaus with rice paddies, palm trees everywhere you look, golden sandy beaches. That could be me describing my perfect island but it's actually me describing Bali.

Perfect backdrop: If you can find anything wrong with this picture of the Gili Islands, tell me!

HIGH AND MIGHTY

Towering over the island is a range of volcanoes responsible for making up this part of the earth's landmass and they play a major role in island life, both agriculturally and spiritually. Tallest of them all is Mount Agung, a powerful symbol for the locals, a peak to be conquered for adventurous visitors and also a warning sign; Agung last erupted in 1963 but recent years have seen volcanic activity on both of Bali's island neighbours and there's no reason to assume that Bali is dormant when it comes to that kind of thing.

You can cook eggs on several of Bali's peaks and see steam emitting from fissures in the rock as a permanent reminder that you only need to scratch the surface to appreciate the potentially explosive situation.

At 3,046 metres (9,994 feet) it's easy to see why Agung has its place in Balinese traditions but it's quite amazing to discover just how much of an influence it has on the Balinese people. The most sacred part of all temples in any complex, the *jeroan*, must face the mountain. The layouts of villages are dictated by the mountain, as are houses and beds, which should be positioned so the head is pointing to the mountain to encourage the flow of life energy. And when it comes to directions, the Balinese traditionally find their way around the island using Agung as a focal point. Who needs north and south, when you have *kaja* (towards the top of the mountain) and *kelod* (towards the sea) Mount Agung is their equivalent of a pole.

Elsewhere, Mount Batur is another great attraction for tourists wishing to see a spectacular sunrise and the area around it is truly epic as there are volcanic craters within craters. Mount Batukaru is the second highest point on the island and is again both popular with tourists and a spiritual icon for the locals. But it's also here where you'll find evidence of the more practical importance of these overbearing peaks as they are key to the island's agricultural success.

All on course: Bali has a surprising number of high-quality golfing options, including Handara in Bedugul.

FIELDS OF DREAMS

Bali has a cooperative water management system, known as *subak*, which is key to its prolific rice growing. It's an irrigation network that begins at the island's highest points, such as the Jatiluwah rice terraces near Mount Batukaru, and flows down through a carefully constructed system to ensure that the water is harvested as carefully as the rice it

helps to grow. The highest fields are flooded first and then a system of canals ensures the water makes its way towards the sea and everyone gets their ration. There are three rice harvests per year here and it makes for an ever-changing and perennially encapsulating landscape. If you had to ask me what is the one thing that defines Bali, that makes it so special, rice fields win hands down. And it's not just the fields themselves, it's the people working a labour intensive farming in the way their ancestors have done for centuries that perfect the picture.

And while rolling vistas of tiered rice paddies can take your breath away, smaller fields can have just as much impact. There's something remarkable about sitting in a modern establishment watching a local up to their knees in water planting seeds. A rice field view can be a key feature for a

Never gets old: Did we mention the fact that there are awesome rice fields everywhere?

Green with envy: There are views to die for at seemingly every turn.

Even in the most developed parts of the island, rice fields are still prevalent. You'll often find one tucked between a five-star hotel and a restaurant.

restaurant and many business owners pay the neighbours not to sell their land in order to retain it.

For the Balinese, rice is not just their key food, it's also sacred and has been since King Petru received some grains as a present that the goddess Sri had to hide to prevent them getting stolen. Sri is the goddess of the rice and you'll see many small temples in the paddies dedicated to her. Like Mount Agung then, rice fields are spiritual and practical for the island's natives where for us interlopers they are merely aesthetically pleasing. Are you spotting a theme? It's one that infuses island life.

Rice is not the only plant to grow prolifically on Bali; indeed it's far from the only crop grown here. Coffee, cacao, bananas, mangoes, mangosteen, rambutan and a year-round strawberry crop make the markets a great place to shop. Chillies and a wide range of spices add to the mix, while grapes also grow in the northern areas. And you'll never be short of coconuts; a *kelapa muda* (young coconut) with the top sliced off makes for a refreshing and healthy drink.

I can't remember the last time I was somewhere and couldn't see a palm tree. I have a personal theory that it's very difficult to be unhappy in places that have palm trees and while that theory has no scientific backing, it surely holds some water. Bamboo is another prolific grower here, and you'll also come across mangroves and banyan trees. There is also a wide variety of flowers, which is rather handy for the Balinese as they use them in their daily offerings and for praying; they consider them a blessing of the gods. The lotus is particularly important to them, while warriors going into battle traditionally wore the hibiscus. Bougainvillea, water lilies, jasmine, frangipani and orchids are highlights of the smorgasbord of flowers you'll see on your travels.

GOING WILD

Wildlife on the island comes in various forms, the most obvious being the lizards that you'll see skittering about your home. While most refer to them by the generic term 'gecko', in reality there are many different types and they coexist happily with humans. Be prepared to find them skulking behind things you pick up or move, and be realistic that they're animals, and animals poo, so you can't expect not to find the odd present left behind.

Bigger monitor lizards can be found around the island, while you'll also come across monkeys, whether in the Monkey Forest at Ubud, hanging out at Uluwatu temple or elsewhere in the forests. For the tweeters (that's birdwatchers, not social media fans) there's some interesting birdlife, including cuckoos, sea eagles and most enticingly the Jalak Bali—a mynah bird exclusive to the island. Oh and there

are bats, lots of bats. Or tame mosquito catchers, as some expats refer to them.

Also indigenous to the island is the Bali Dog. You'll find various other species all over the island and I find the human-canine relationship here fascinating. They're generally left to their own devices and not 'owned' by anyone in particular. When a rabies epidemic occurred, the official solution was just to cull them; it took intervention by Westerners to implement a vaccination programme. So they do love them, don't really own them, don't think twice about knocking them off as a short-term solution to disease and, in certain areas, eat them. Eating dog is not illegal, but the way the *warungs* — family restaurants — that sell them procure and kill them usually is. A curious relationship indeed.

Any talk of flora and fauna in these parts would not be complete without talk of what lies underneath. Bali is a divers' paradise with some beautiful reefs populated by turtles and an army of marine life. In the right season you'll be able to get up close and personal with manta rays, while the huge mola-mola fish is another creature that will entice you into the water. Dolphins also like the waters around Bali so there's plenty of life under the waves to inspire you to get into the water.

Equally to talk of flora and fauna, climate is key. This is a tropical island, lying just eight degrees south of the equator. This allows for temperature that remains relatively constant all year. The average temperature barely fluctuates, from a low of 26°C (79°F) in January to a high of 28°C (82°F) in May. There are microclimates and you'll notice a difference between coastal areas and those at a higher altitude. You're unlikely to ever need a coat though. (If you have one spare the Balinese will probably appreciate it—you'll get used to them wearing coats and gloves on a moped even in the most scorching heat as they attempt to protect themselves from the sun.)

All of which isn't to say the weather is always the same—far from it. But where most countries will have four seasons, Bali has two: wet (November–April) and dry (May–October). And when it's wet in Bali it's really wet. Wet in terms of rain, wet in terms of humidity and wet in terms of sweat. It starts to get humid before the rains come so when they do it is a blessed relief. Where some tropical climates have a predictable rain pattern of an hour a day at certain times of day, in Bali there's no such predictability. It rains when it wants, for as long as it wants and like it really, really means it. The roads flood easily although there are drains and dry quickly when the rain stops. If all that sounds terrible there are few things nicer than sitting in your villa listening and watching tropical rain—it's only if you have to actually move anywhere that it becomes a pain. And even then it is a small price worth paying for the dry season.

A seemingly never-ending six to seven months where clouds are but memories, rain is something you vaguely remember and the dry heat is permanently pleasant. Whether due to climate change or not, the rainy season in the last couple of years has arrived late and stayed late, albeit not late enough to leave the island without genuine fears of a water shortage.

We've been up the hills, across the fields, discussed what grows from the ground, what lives on the ground and the weather. All of which leaves one key geographical feature of Bali until last, which for the majority is a primary concern: the beaches. For most visitors this means the 15-kilometre (9-mile) stretch of dark sand from Kuta running north past Legian and Seminyak into Canggu. Keep heading north and the sand gets darker and darker. It's not the only place on the island you'll find black sand beaches that have a type of beauty all of their own, but they do burn your feet rather quickly. One of my favourite 'you don't see that every day' moments was at the Alila Soori resort watching a cow amble down the black sand beach. Elsewhere you'll find pebble beaches, surf beaches, secluded beaches and white sand beaches. To say there's a beach for everyone would sound twee, but would also be fairly accurate.

BLOOD, SWEAT AND TEARS

It's not hard to work out why Bali is one of the world's great tourist destinations, endearing enough to tempt European travellers to put up with the long journey and perennially popular with Australians attracted to one of its closest warm weather destinations, though increasingly popular with Chinese and other Asian visitors as well. While the history of its tourism is a story in itself, the history of the island is one of mass killings, mass suicides, invasions, occupation, pillaging and warring dynasties—a familiar story of politics, religion and greed. It may sound like I'm describing the latest series of TV show *Game of Thrones*, but it neatly sums up the history of this romantic, beautiful and peaceful island that attracts tourists by the million from around the globe. There are few countries or provinces in the world that don't have their fair share of bloody history, yet such is the beauty and strategic importance of this jewel in Indonesia's crown it's unsurprising to discover that it's long been considered a prize worth fighting for.

You'll have to forgive me for dealing with a large collection of seismic events with little more than a soupçon of brevity but there's a lot to get through, so let's crack on. According to Robert Pringle in his *A Short History of Bali* there are three important features of Balinese history: the development of irrigated agriculture, the adoption of Indian religion and the growth of tourism. While these are undoubtedly important, and it seems clear that the former was vital for creating wealth in the little recorded early history of Bali, it's the continual interfering by outsiders that needs to be appreciated to get a handle on how the island has evolved.

NOSY NEIGHBOURS

The first people to come poking their heads into Bali's business were the neighbouring Javanese, which is hardly surprising when you consider the short distance across the Bali Strait. In the early centuries of the second millennium various Javanese rulers came and went as power struggles saw control of the island swapping hands between Javanese and Balinese ruling houses.

In the 1300s the Majapahit Empire based in Java successfully brought much of the Indonesian archipelago, including Bali, under its control. This set the scene for a strong influence of Javanese culture into Bali in the forms of architecture, dance and theatre. And it wasn't just culture that Java exported, but religion. The Majapahit was Hindu and this became the predominant religion in Bali. But in the mid-1400s a religious sea change was in the air and as Islam spread throughout Indonesia, it signalled the beginning of the end for the Majapahit Empire. But while this swept though Indonesia, for some reason (there are several hypotheses, but none satisfactory) this spread of Islam did not cross over the Bali Strait and as a result the influence of Majapahit actually increased in Bali. As the Empire crumbled there was a mass exodus of intelligentsia and aristocracy from Java to Bali. As the *Lonely Planet Guide to Bali & Lombok* states, "Artists, dancers, musicians and actors also fled to

Bali at this time, and the island experienced an explosion of cultural activities." For this reason, Wikipedia explains, "the vivid, rich and festive Balinese culture is considered as one of Majapahit's legacy." It could be said that while the Empire died, it has been forever retained in Bali.

There followed a relatively long period of history when Bali was left to its own devices. Again I'm not intimating that nothing happened, but in terms of drawing a line between the past and the present in a succinct fashion the next momentous happenings involved contact with Europeans, led by the Dutch. (There is talk of Portuguese and Spanish expeditions sighting the island and claims that Sir Francis Drake actually paid a visit in 1580, but they are relatively incidental to this tale.) Cornelis de Houtman was the leader of an expedition that discovered a new sea route between Europe and what is now Indonesia and became Bali's first European 'tourist' in 1597. In typically arrogant European style, he christened the island "Young Holland". Two of his crew fell in love with the island so much they refused to leave—a magnetic appeal Bali has never lost.

GOING DUTCH

While de Houtman was the first Dutch visitor he wasn't to be the last, but it would be a long time before the Dutch had designs on ruling the island. A second expedition arrived in 1601 and a short-lived trading post was set up in 1620, but generally the island was left to deal with private traders, the major products being opium and slaves. Dutch activity at this period in time was carried out by the Dutch East Indies Company with tacit approval from the country's rulers. The Dutch East India Company was arguably the world's first multi-national company and was purely interested in profits and trade, hence it pretty much left Bali alone in favour of other more profitable ventures. They did have a common enemy though, in the Javanese Mataram Sultanate and there was talk of Bali-Dutch alliances in their separate fights against the Mataram, but they never eventuated to anything. In the late 1600s Bali split into nine minor kingdoms that continually fought among themselves, but we must fast-forward a couple of hundred years to get our teeth into the real developments as European imperialism came to the fore.

It's worth taking a moment here to refer to our friend Robert Pringle who writes of Bali before colonial rule: "It was a complex setting, replete with regional variations, charismatic individuals and constant political change. Pre-Colonial Bali bore little resemblance to the idyllic vision of later European

visitors. Warfare, disease and natural disaster were all commonplace. Slavery and drug addiction were among the less savoury practices."

Dutch priorities changed from purely business to colonialism as a result of the Dutch East Indies Company going bankrupt in 1800 and its interests being taken over by the Dutch Government. Once the French and British interfering were seen off, that government set about making the area its own and created the Dutch East Indies—the country now known as Indonesia. And that included taking control of Bali.

Dutch intervention came in the form of three campaigns in 1846, 1848 and 1849. While the Balinese repelled the first two attempts, the Dutch established administration over the north of Bali after 1849. Their justification for the campaign was to eradicate opium smuggling, slavery and the plundering of shipwrecks.

In 1894 the Dutch took advantage of internal struggles to expand its control to include neighbouring Lombok and Karangesem (Eastern Bali). Going into the 20th century, the Dutch intervened in southern Bali, first in 1906 and then a successful campaign in 1908 that heralded the Dutch finally taking complete control of the island. While there were serious misgivings over the way the Dutch had taken control of the island, it had a positive long-term effect as they instigated an Ethical Policy to make amends. While administrative control was left to the Dutch, local control over religion and culture remained.

Dutch rule instigated lots of positive change and the seedlings of tourism were planted. According to *A Short History of Bali*: "In 1914 the first tourist brochure to include images of Bali appeared. In 1923 Dutch passenger ships began serving Singaraja, and in 1928 the government guest house in Denpasar was upgraded and reopened as the Bali Hotel, the island's first and for many years only real hotel."

The beginnings of tourism can be seen there, but there was still a series of traumatic periods for the island to go through to get where it is today. The first of those was Japanese occupation. In February 1942 Bali was handed over to the Japanese as they swept through south-east Asia, but if the Dutch rule had been short (just 34 years had passed since their complete occupation began) the Japanese residency was destined to be even shorter—as World War II ended, the Japanese ceded control. But the end of that war was only the beginning of the fight for Indonesia.

WAR STORIES

The Dutch assumed that its ex-colony would simply come back under its control. But the world had changed dramatically and independence was the name of the game globally and nowhere more so than Indonesia where the pro-independence movement had been on the rise for many years. So when the Dutch returned to assert their authority in 1946 they found resistance; a resistance armed with the Japanese weapons that had been left behind. The Balinese resistance was wiped out and the island was named as one of 13 districts in the State of East Indonesia proclaimed by the Dutch, but this new state had a rival in the Republic of Indonesia formed by Indonesia's first President, Sukarno. He had been a leader of the nationalist movement during Dutch colonialism and ironically it was the Japanese that opened the door for him to eventually take power as he supported the Japanese war effort in exchange for Japanese approval in spreading nationalist ideas.

The Indonesian Declaration of Independence came on August 17, 1945, but a four-year battle ensued with the Dutch until the Nationalist forces finally prevailed, as Pringle explains: "The handover of sovereignty to the Republic of Indonesia took place on 27 December 1949. The war for Indonesian Independence had cost Bali about 2,000 casualties, of whom roughly one third died fighting on the Dutch side."

But if Indonesia and the island of Bali finally thought peace had arrived, they were to be brutally mistaken. That illusion of peace was first shattered on Bali in 1963, when Mount Agung erupted, killing thousands, creating an economic disaster and leading to multitudes of Balinese being displaced and shunted to other parts of Indonesia. But while natural disasters can account for thousands of deaths, the human race usually assumes much more deadliness when it comes to wiping out its own race. On October 1, 1965, there was an attempted coup d'etat. It was quickly put down but although evidence is still unclear as to its precise origins, the ruling party immediately associated the coup with the Indonesian Communist Party (PKI) and used it as an excuse to begin a campaign of mass killing that affected the whole country. Pringle describes the tragic reality of this period on Bali:

"Whole villages, including children, took part in an island-wide witch-hunt for Communists who were slashed and clubbed and chopped to death, by communal consent. Whole villages that had made the fatal mistake of embracing Communism were wiped out… Night after night flared red over Bali as villages went up in flames and thousand of Communists, or people said to be Communists, were hunted down and killed. Knowledgeable sources say 40,000 Balinese were killed in two weeks of butchery. Estimates have gone as high as 80,000... As one Balinese told me, 'When people were killed in batches of less than ten, nobody even bothered to keep count.' "

The ensuing half century has seen a mass invasion of Bali of a different kind: tourism. The tourist boom really started to take off in the early 1970s and while it has bought obvious benefits to the island in terms of roads, money, infrastructure, employment and more, it has also placed a huge amount of pressure on that infrastructure and issues such as overdevelopment, traffic, pollution and other ecological and sociological problems have come to the fore. These issues were exacerbated when the island was dragged into geopolitical disputes and the Bali bombings in 2002 put the island on the map for different reasons. Another attack in 2005 also affected tourism, but it has since recovered and year-on-year numbers of tourists continue to grow.

Thankfully and remarkably, after such an onslaught of both warring and peaceful intruders, Bali has managed to retain its culture and to this day remains the only predominantly Hindu island in Indonesia. As Adrian Vickers puts it in his introduction to Bali Chronicles by William Hanna: "In Bali's case, tourism has helped to reinforce a separate sense of Balinese identity, and given Balinese players in Indonesian society the means by which to support their island's idea of uniqueness."

It's an amazing achievement that the Balinese culture has survived so many incursions and interruptions and ironically this provides yet another attraction for tourists. It is somewhat ironic then that Bali's current battle is to retain its culture and identity in the face of modernism and the inexorable growth of the tourism industry whose tentacles reach ever further through the island. But while there are undoubtedly less rice fields, more roads, hotels, advertising and restaurants, much of Bali remains completely unspoilt and its tumultuous history suggests Bali will find a way to both survive and prosper.

The White King of Bali

While it was the Dutch who were most closely associated with the island during the 19th century, it was a Dane who will remain synonymous with the island in that period. Meds Lange was a Danish trader who settled on Bali after a life at sea and an aborted attempt at settling on Lombok. He maintained great relationships with the local rajas (rulers) and that enabled him to develop a successful import and export business. During the Dutch campaigns in the 1840s it was Lange who was continually relied upon to mediate between the Dutch and the rajas as he retained the trust of both. As a result of his work he was appointed High Commissioner by the Balinese and awarded knight of the Order of the Netherlands Lion by the Dutch. Sadly the wars had a detrimental impact on trade as Balinese crops suffered and Dutch blockades affected his business. But his legacy will live on forever.

Puputan

Puputan is a Balinese term that means mass suicide. Sadly it is a recurring theme in Balinese history. The first occurrence we discovered comes during the 1849 Dutch intervention when the Raja of Buleleng and his confidantes invoked it. In 1906 it was the royal house of Badung. When a large Dutch force landed at Sanur and marched on the palace they met no resistance. Upon arriving at the palace a procession of members of the royal household met them and the Raja stepped forward and signalled a priest to stab him with a dagger. A number of similar killings ensued until either a stray shot or an attack led the Dutch to open fire. By the time the killing had finished, 1,000 Balinese lay dead. Two years later a similar event took place when the Dutch walked on Klungkung Palace.

The *puputan* had an unforeseen side effect on colonial policy as Pringle explains: "The political impact of the *puputan* on the evolving colonial order was significant. They were a huge embarrassment to the Dutch... (who) were supposedly imposing their rule to do away with barbarities such as slavery and widow burning." This led to the Ethical Policy outlined above.

When the Dutch fought the Balinese in the aftermath of World War II, history repeated itself as a Balinese freedom army led by Colonel I Gusti Ngurah Rai in 1946 was wiped out in similar circumstances.

Bali and the Napoleonic wars

In the early 1800s Napoleon took control of the Netherlands (he called it the Kingdom of Holland—a name many still mistakenly use today) and Bali was asked to support a Franco-Dutch administration in defence against the British who were also intent on exploiting the area. As Java fell to the British soon afterwards any alliance was never really instigated.

With Java under its control, inevitably the British turned their attentions to Bali but in its five-year domination of the area the British never made much headway into Bali—indeed the Balinese actually took the fight to them and attacked the British in Java at one point. At the end of the Napoleonic Wars Britain ceded the East Indies to the Netherlands again and faded out of the picture as Bali once again found itself the subject of Dutch desires. (One legacy of British rule that still stands is that Indonesians drive on the left.)

Timeline of intervention

1597: Expedition led by Cornelis de Houtman lands on Bali
1601: Second expedition lands on Bali
1620: Short-lived trading post set up by Dutch
1800: Dutch East Indies Company goes bankrupt
1846: First Dutch Campaign
1848: Second Dutch Campaign
1849: Third Dutch Campaign—Dutch take control of northern Bali
1894: Dutch take control of Lombok and Karangesem
1908: Dutch take control of whole island
1914: First tourist brochure with images of Bali
1928: Bali Hotel opens—Bali's first hotel
1942: Island handed over to Japanese
1945: Indonesian Declaration of Independence
1949: Dutch hand over sovereignty to Indonesia

Mulyati Gozali and her daughter Evy had been regular visitors to Bali from their home in Jakarta, but it was a rare trip to the north of the island that was to change their destiny and lead to the creation of the island's only 100 per cent Balinese winery.

They made a trip to the Buleleng region in northern Bali during grape harvesting time, but while some grapes were being sold on the street, many ripe grapes still hung on the vines while others were already overripe. After quizzing the vineyard owners it transpired that the money realised from the crop was not even high enough to pay for the pickers to take the grapes off the vine. This did not make sense to the business-minded pair (Mulyati is an accountant, while Evy studied economics and engineering) and they soon hatched a plan to change the farmers' lot.

Their response was two-pronged. Firstly to set up a farmers' collective, Asteroid Vineyards, that took a co-operative approach to helping local grape growers. But what could they do with all those grapes? The answer was obvious. Make wine. They set up the Sababay winery and where grapes used to rot they now find their way to restaurant tables in Bali and beyond.

CHAPTER 3

THE PEOPLE OF BALI

I'LL STICK MY NECK OUT AND SAY THIS ABOUT THE BALINESE.....

> *[It] might have you mistaking hedonism, not Hindusim, for the local religion. But scratch the surface and you'll find that Bali's soul remains unchanged.*

– Lonely Planet: Bali & Lombok

STANDING ON CEREMONY

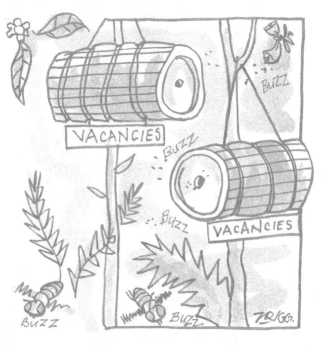

Before delving deep into the life and times of the Balinese people it's important to consider that the nature of migration here is not limited to Western expats seeking a relaxed way of life; Indonesians are also attracted here in huge numbers and the main reason for that is you. Because of the sheer numbers of tourists and expats that populate Bali at any given time, it is a jobs honeypot that attracts Indonesia's worker bees. Tourism generates so much employment that internal migration is huge and this means that you'll encounter Indonesians from different islands with different cultural backgrounds.

It's not just employment that initiates this internal migration; many are attracted to Bali for exactly the same reasons you are. The party scene draws younger people, and the beaches and laidback way of life are equally enticing whether you were born in Jakarta or Johannesburg. Indeed it can be more attractive for Indonesians owing to the huge cultural divide; as the only Hindu island in a predominantly Muslim country, Bali is a beacon of free spirit and hedonism in an otherwise strict territory. An example of how this works came in 2015 when the Indonesian government passed a law banning the sale of alcohol in minimarts; Bali was immediately granted an exemption. The reasoning was that it would unfairly punish small businesses and have a negative impact on tourism; the effect was to increase Bali's appearance of being free from the strictures prevalent throughout the rest of Indonesia. (That doesn't extend as far as drugs; the death penalty or a long stretch in prison awaits those who get caught with them anywhere in Indonesia.) And it's not just about alcohol, but lifestyle. All religions are respected, while attitudes to homosexuality are much more open-minded than in the rest of the country.

As a result, you will encounter people from different parts of Indonesia, but the large majority of 'locals' you meet will be just that: Balinese locals. And for that you can count yourself fortunate. While the island has metamorphosed over the last 20 years and there are legitimate concerns that the expansion and continual development of new hotels, restaurants and bars are somehow ripping the soul out of Bali, the attitudes of the people haven't seemed to change much. There's no doubting that there are more buildings and less trees and rice fields than there used to be, but one thing seems to remain the same: the Balinese people and their view of what is going on around them.

I sometimes feel it borders on bemusement; that all the craziness going on around them really doesn't pierce their life bubbles. Indeed I think if we all upped sticks tomorrow and the island emptied of its various interlopers, the collective would merely shrug its shoulders and get on with life. Because while many in this world are constantly looking for something else, for a new adventure, for new experiences, for new cars and new clothes, the Balinese seem to have everything they need in their religion, their family and their village.

If that sounds overly simplistic, it's not. Their lives are dedicated to those three strands and the satisfaction they get from them seems to be more than enough to make them happy. And happy they almost always are, always ready with a smile, happy to chat, content to talk English but excited if you make an effort to converse in their language. To say they are the nicest people in the world would be a ridiculous generalisation but I will stick my neck out and say this: if the people of the rest of the world had the same attitudes as the Balinese, we'd live on a much nicer planet. Not that they are entirely perfect, as we shall discover, but overall they're a wonderfully warm people.

Religion is key to the Balinese way of life and it plays an extraordinarily large part in their activities from birth until death. This is obvious initially by the number of temples — Bali may be known as the 'island of a thousand *puras*' (temples), but one estimate I read puts the number of them at 20,000, another at 50,000, and in truth nobody has an accurate figure.

The reason for this is that we're not talking about temples as you would talk about churches or mosques. There are communal temples, but additionally every building has one. That's every house, every hotel, every restaurant, but it doesn't stop there. You'll also find them on beaches, hillsides, in fields, rivers and in the middle of roundabouts. They are everywhere.

As the website www.balix.com puts it: "Bali is a floating shrine, where all the homes are temples and all the temples homes."

Stacked up: The temple designs are varied but always impressive.

And if you think this is evidence of their dedication, then watching the Balinese go about their daily lives reinforces the point and then some. Put simply, life is pretty much dedicated to honouring the gods and appeasing demons. There are many gods to honour and that's pretty time-consuming. A classic example is Brahma—the god of moving metal objects. If someone buys a new car or moped, they have a ceremony in Brahma's honour. That's the level of dedication we're looking at.

For an outsider it is incredibly confusing trying to unravel this religion but then even the Balinese don't understand everything implicitly. Theirs is "a rather complex mix between worshipping nature and the ancestors, Buddhist and Hindu practises (sic) and the diabolical beliefs of the tantric cults... you must find this very complicated, and we do too actually." (*My Life in Bali*, Sandrine Soimaud) In an attempt to simplify it, the Balinese believe there are three parts to the universe: the negative that belongs to the demons, the highest is the

Carved up: You'll soon notice that the Balinese are very keen on sculpting.

domain of the gods while humans reside in the neutral. It is every human's role to act in an appropriate manner to retain balance in the cosmos at the expense of personal desires.

Not that the Balinese have to eschew desire completely. But life is about achieving balance between four goals of life: desire (*kama*), wealth (*artha*), virtue (*dharma*) and the final objective of merging

oneself into the universe (*moksa*).
It's why when it comes to
a ceremony in a Balinese
village, the wealthy will make
the biggest contributions.
These dedications inspire
every part of Balinese life.

To say these offerings are ubiquitous would be something of an understatement. There's nowhere they won't put on and they quickly become part and parcel of your surroundings so you almost become oblivious to them.

It begins on a daily basis; every
morning and evening offerings are
made to both the gods and the demons.
The gods' goodies are placed on raised shrines and contain
flower petals and food treats, sprinkled with holy water and
adorned with incense. The demons are less picky so the
offerings you see for them are less dainty. It always raises
a smile for me when I see people have placed cigarettes
in there.

Then there are temple ceremonies (*odalan*) that occur
every year on the anniversary of the date the temple
was consecrated. (Note that
a Balinese year only has
210 days, so that's three
ceremonies every year of the
Roman calendar.) So if you
remember those thousands of
temples we discussed, each
has a ceremony every year,
while the fifth, tenth, thirtieth
and centennial ceremonies
are bigger than normal.
And everyone associated
with those temples will be
expected to attend.

Offering up: The gods must be
pleased and offered to twice
a day.

Let's throw in life ceremonies: birth, death, weddings sure, but there are also half a dozen ceremonies within the first six months of a babies' arrival. And a puberty ceremony. And a teeth-filing ceremony… the list goes on. And we haven't even begun to explore the big annual ceremonies that can literally bring the island to a standstill.

Add it all up and it's hard to work out where the Balinese find time to do anything other than attend ceremonies. Add in work and family and life is pretty much complete.

If the power of religion is strong here, then the power of community is equally important. Many Balinese, especially in rural areas, barely leave the confines of their village throughout their lives. Those who leave, whether for reasons of marriage or work, return regularly throughout the year for various reasons (most of which, unsurprisingly, involve ceremonies). Everyone is expected to play their part towards

the greater collective and this is often linked to your position in society. The more money you have, the more you're expected to donate to village activities.

Knowing all this, it's unsurprising to discover the importance of family in everyday life. As we've already highlighted, every family compound has a temple and through this individuals

Standing on ceremony: When the Balinese celebrate, the traffic stops.

have a very strong connection to their home. Multiple generations live together; when sons marry they don't move out, their wives move in. It may sounds like an idyllic comingling of society, but on one visit to a family compound I questioned why there were two kitchens, only to find out that one was for the mother and one for the daughter-in-law so they didn't argue about how to do things. It was almost reassuring to hear that the harmony does have its limits and it brought a wry smile to my face. You can appease the demons, but not necessarily the mother-in-law.

Cooking is just one of the roles of females in Balinese society. They are very much the carers and preparers of food but this isn't restricted to the home, which is why you'll see many cafes and stalls managed by women. And while it may suggest that this is a world where men do the tough work and women keep house it's not necessarily the case. While men generally rule village affairs and take responsibility for growing the crops, women do a lot of the heavy lifting, both literally and metaphorically. Manual labour is every bit a female preserve here, while at the other end of the spectrum they also have responsibility for preparing and carrying out the daily offerings to the gods and demons. Equality it isn't, nor does it fit to antiquated, conventional Western stereotypes of the 'fairer sex'.

All of that is for adult life, but before reaching that stage, the Balinese go through many rites of passage leading, inevitably, to more ceremonies. The first comes before the baby is even born, when the mother is six months pregnant. A further one comes when the umbilical cord falls off, then after 42 days when the negative spirits have left the body, then after 105 days (three Balinese months) when the baby is named. Then there's the first birthday celebration (210 days). Other ceremonies include loss of the first tooth, but that's not the only tooth-related ceremony and the more squeamish among you might want to look away now. At the end of adolescence a tooth filing ceremony is held and the canines are filed down to match the molars. Weddings and cremations are somewhat more universal and as with all ceremonies the whole village will get involved on each occasion.

Historically there has been little internal migration or widening of work, but as the island has changed, so have the opportunities available to Balinese people. They now filter through every level of the service industry and beyond; they own businesses and they work their way up in businesses.

So there has been change, but when the village calls the Balinese answer. Anyone who has Balinese staff will know all too well that if there's a ceremony in the village there's no questioning the right of the employee to have the day off. It's not optional, it's not something they ask permission for (if you're luck you'll get a day's notice), and it's something that is non-negotiable. It's the way things are done.

For all their tolerance and community spirit it doesn't always extend to interference from outside. There was drama in my first villa when the landlord replaced our Balinese pool boy with a Javanese guy; so much so that the move was reversed within days after some behind-the-scenes machinations. I've heard many similar stories.

And the Balinese are not against a bit of pettiness when it suits them. Not long after the pool boy saga, the main access point to that same villa was blocked off when the local landowner decided to do a Donald Trump and build a lovely wall down his entire 'gang' or laneway, blocking off car access to our property. It benefited nobody, inconvenienced us, reduced the value of our landlord's villa and it was done and without a word of warning. The first we knew of it was when our *pembantu* (helper) came in and told us they were building a wall. When my landlord offered to rent the six feet as the main entrance to our home from him he merely shrugged and said it was his right to build there, giving up the opportunity to make money for nothing, for what reason I can't fathom. The fact they dug the foundation for this wall on Christmas Eve and didn't bother coming to actually build it for several more days merely added to the sense that this was petty barrier building rather than strategic construction.

Another side of the Balinese (and Indonesians in general) came to the fore during that episode—that of practical problem solving. Actually first there was the bit where they struggle to realise where is a problem in the first place, then comes the part when they realise and do something about it.

The only other access point to the villas was one we'd never previously used as it involved a narrow 'gang' and a set of stairs. When I pointed out to the hired labourers that my moped was now stranded between a wall foundation and a set of stairs that mopeds are not designed to negotiate, they merely shrugged their shoulders, got out their hammers and smashed the stairs into pieces in order to make them into a ramp. I had to point out what was obvious, but it was a very Balinese way of dealing with things; they are incredibly practical problem solvers, which is something I admire, having lived in societies where the slightest hint of damage necessitates the calling of a specialist to fix it. This is an island of DIY experts, whether it's working on machines, homes or

entrances to villas. Having said all that, the phrase "built to last" is something of an anathema. The 'pavements' are a continual reminder of that fact.

But away from the inter-island rivalries and interesting approach to their even closer neighbours, the Balinese are incredibly nice, tolerant, welcoming and friendly. They allow Westerners to live here with little complaint and seem happy on the whole to share their island with us. The fascinating part is going to be watching the island and its natives evolve over the next 20 years. A lot of Balinese have become very rich on the back of the Western invasion, selling land for significant amounts of money. One friend tells the story of the man he bought his land off; he knows he sold several plots and must be pretty wealthy, especially in Balinese terms. But he still lives in his basic accommodation, cleaning every morning with cold water out of a bucket. Selling the land seems to have had no effect on his lifestyle because personal desires are largely irrelevant. My old landlord told a similar story of following a man who "looked homeless" into the ATM (not at the same time), only to look at the receipt slip he left behind and discover he had an absolute fortune in the bank. Wealth has come to the Balinese but they seem to have little real need for it. Whether the next generation continues along that theme or becomes more consumer driven will be fascinating to watch; for now I enjoy living somewhere that isn't driven by greed, but by spirituality and devotion.

The powers that be

Bali is one big collection of villages and life is dictated by the people who run those villages. You might think when you're in the heart of Kuta or Seminyak that this doesn't apply but it is every bit as relevant there as in the middle of rural Bali. Locals regularly meet to plan, celebrate and make decisions and central to this is the *banjar*—a type of local neighbourhood organisation. There are over 3,500 of these on the island deciding everything from what will happen for certain ceremonies to which businesses can operate within its confines. Do not underestimate the power of the *banjar*; it can close businesses on a whim and is the centre of influence. The *banjar* is made up of married men and all people in the village are expected to do their duty as it decrees. On the day I wrote this paragraph I went out of my house to discover traffic chaos because there was a wedding taking place. The *banjar* closed Jalan Seminyak, one of the island's busiest thoroughfares, for the wedding to take place. The movement of others is deemed way less important than the opportunity for people to celebrate where they want to and that's typical of the Balinese attitude and approach.

My favourite thing about Bali is the culture. With the little offerings everywhere, it's a breath of fresh air. The people make the place. Even though you have all this development going on, if you sit and ignore that, you still see in front of a new 300-bedroom hotel the Balinese doing their offerings, and I think that makes it unique.

– Luke Stockley, owner, Jemme restaurant and jewellery store

Rough justice

There is crime in Bali. This is hardly surprising for a place that attracts so many Westerners people are looking to take advantage of. I have been a victim myself, relieved of my wallet and phone after getting in the wrong cab at the wrong time after one too many glasses of wine to find a few thousand dollars totted up on various cards by the time I realised.

Yet this is at odds with a world where many villas or family compounds facilitate 'open living'. I have no door to the main part of my villa and this is common, which means that there are untold numbers of televisions, DVD players and kitchen appliances easily available to anyone who can be bothered to scale a wall. In some ways it's a burglar's paradise and yet that particular crime does not seem to be an issue. It's more the opportunistic targeting of individuals that is, with single females particularly targeted for bag snatching.

And yet this also often inspires a heavy type of social justice. Because those of a more honest bent are proud of their island and protective of its visitors, woe betide anyone who attempts a bag snatch in view of the locals. I have seen it happen myself; once looking up to see an Indonesian lad fleeing an angry mob after a bag snatch attempt in central Seminyak. He tried to get away on a scooter but got stuck in traffic and so decided to abandon it and continue on foot. The scooter was brought back to the scene of the crime with all the pomp and ceremony of a toppled Saddam statue after the Iraqi dictator's reign was ended and the locals took turns kicking it—although I'm not sure what that really achieved.

The other thing they took turns kicking was the perpetrator when they finally caught up with him. Justice is meted out violently here; indeed one petty thief was actually killed around the corner from my house just a couple of weeks before that incident. One can appreciate the desire to seek justice for those that are wronged, but the levels of violence involved can be truly disturbing in what is generally perceived as a place of peace and harmony.

What's in a name?

Once you've met a few of the locals you'll be slightly confused about the fact that so many of them have the same name. You'll probably be even more confused by the fact that many men and women have the same name. That's because there are only a handful of first names in Bali. The first-born is always called Wayan, or occasionally Putu, regardless of gender. There is an alternative, Gede, but this can only be used for males. The second child is called Made or more rarely Kadek; the third Nyoman or Komang. Fourth is Ketut. And fifth? Well, simply go back to the start and it's Wayan, Putu or Gede again. This means it is perfectly feasible to have a family where the father is called Wayan, the mother is called Wayan and the first-born is, you guessed it, Wayan.

There are no real family names; last names are bestowed dependent on characteristics the child shows or the parents would like the child to show. It is this name that locals tend to use among themselves more often, but they will often introduce themselves as Ketut, Wayan etc. If you meet an Indonesian who does not have one of the above names then the chances are they hail from a different island.

CHAPTER 4

FITTING INTO
SOCIETY

> ❝This little group of people in Bali have become my family. And we must take care of our families, wherever we find them.❞

> – **Elizabeth Gilbert**, *Eat, Pray, Love*

RUBBING ALONG NICELY

Balinese and expats co-exist quite happily but realistically their lives are very different. When it came to writing this chapter I felt somewhat sad to realise how little I had integrated into 'Balinese society' as a whole. But then the more I thought about it the more that seemed inevitable, rather than something I should be ashamed of. And as I asked my expat friends a similar story emerged. If you've read Chapter Three it will become immediately apparent that there are several reasons why the expat community exists more alongside than intermingled with the Balinese community.

Firstly, there's a cultural gulf. The life of a Western expat compared to that of a Balinese person couldn't be more different. Where religion, community and family are the cornerstones of Balinese existence, expats tend to be more about travel, adventure and transience. Expat lifestyle is also quite indulgent, revolving around lots of socialising, eating out and the odd bit of alcohol consumption (OK, quite a lot of alcohol consumption generally). All of which are not exactly anathema to the Balinese, but hanging outside a *warung* sharing a Bintang isn't the same as cocktails and dinner at one of Bali's multitudinous restaurants.

Then there's a financial reality. Every expat is rich. Even the poor ones. Wages for locals are very low so even if they did aspire to the expat lifestyle—and few of them really do anyway—they couldn't afford it. You'll see rich Jakartans in

The great equaliser: The beach is a great place to meet people, be it locals or foreigners.

high-end restaurants or trendy bars, but you won't see many Balinese in them.

Thirdly, there's the nature of expat existence, specifically their employment. Very few expats in Bali have what I would term a 'proper job' — by which I mean one where you get up every morning, commute to an office and join your colleagues for a day's graft in the office. I work remotely, one friend is a freelance photographer, one is a DJ, one has a property business, while another is a self-employed architect. Nearly everyone here seems to be self-employed, contracting or a business owner. So generally people don't have the day-to-day interaction with local staff. And if you do happen to work with them, the cultural differences might make it difficult to engage in the same way you might otherwise. The 'after work drink' that is the cornerstone of many workplace social crossovers is not going to be a regular occurrence here.

All of which is not to say there is no interaction at all, but there's certainly not as much as you might expect where cultures are more closely aligned. One passion I do share with many Balinese is that of *sepak bola* (football) and we often enjoy games with and against local teams. I don't know a *bule* who isn't happy to pay for a local to enjoy a game on the same pitch and it's a great way to share an experience. (The word '*bule*' is one you need to know. It's a catch-all term for white foreigners, generally used with affection, sometimes derogatively.) Not that you always have to pay for a pitch as nature has provided a perfectly good one on that huge stretch of beach the main tourist areas are built upon. Every night groups of locals create pitches and do battle and they're usually very open to interlopers who want to get involved. Indeed the beach is a great place for people to mix, or at least enjoy

I love going to the beach on a Sunday—most Balinese work six-day weeks so Sunday is their day to enjoy and I always think this is the day they reclaim 'their' beach.

simultaneously. It's a great equaliser of a place, the beach. The waves, the sun and the sand belong to nobody and can be enjoyed by all equally, no matter their social background or fiscal status.

But back to that financial disparity and the nature of employment. It should come as no surprise to discover that most interactions between *bules* and Balinese come as a result of Balinese working for expats, whether in the role of *pembantus* (helpers), pool boys (always boys for some reason), gardeners or servers in restaurants, bars and shops. I try my hardest to have a laugh and a joke with them, to be friendly and ask questions about them: where they are from, whether they have family. And as we have already seen, they are generally very friendly in return.

When I walk outside to start my day every morning I feel happy that the birds are chirping, the sun is shining, the weather is warm and that I know the gardener will be somewhere with a "*selamat pagi*, *apa kabar*" to start my morning. (Good morning, How are you?) Not all people are as interested in interacting, but most are and this creates a bond. Yes there is an employer-employee relationship but it is not that of master and servant. Many *pembantus* become almost part of their adopted families and end up travelling with them. And even short-term relationships formed by tourists here can endure; I recently delivered a gift of money from one Australian friend to a nanny who had looked after her kids for a week and found herself in some financial difficulty.

Outside of the home there's the myriad waiting staff and shopkeepers, mechanics and handymen you'll deal with. There are quite a few Balinese people working various cafes who know that 'Pak Paul' (Mr Paul) likes to start his day with a cappuccino. That's in the places I frequent regularly, but

one downside to living here is the fact that until you prove otherwise, everyone you meet will assume you are on holiday.

The Balinese will always be interested in your background story, but rarely judge you for any of it. Where you come from, what you do, how long you have been here and so on are standard questions, but these are asked out of interest and not with a view to prejudice. Live and let live seems to be very much the order of the day and it's an attitude that

When chatting with the locals they will often enquire of a couple whether they are married and if they have children. A word of advice: whatever the reality of your situation, just say yes to both questions if it's a casual conversation. The Balinese struggle to get their heads round couples that are not married and, if anything, they struggle even more with the concept of not having children. My ex found this out when she ended up having a full-on argument with a taxi driver after trying to explain that she didn't want any offspring. Even for those who are planning to have kids at some point, but not yet, the Balinese will just assume you are trying for them anyway—it's just a natural way of life for them.

expats generally reflect back. Being surrounded by Balinese people, seeing their way of life, their general state of happiness and well-being is instructive and rubs off on those around them. I like to think we all learn something from that—I certainly have.

There is almost always a change in attitude when you explain to someone that you live in Bali, especially if you are able to transmit that information in the local tongue.

If there's one scenario whereby there is a mixing of cultures then it's where Cupid interferes. One of my good friends recently proposed to his Balinese girlfriend and amid all the banter about how he will now have to go through the teeth-filing ceremony we mentioned in Chapter Three, and while he is trying to work his way through the minefield of what is expected of him, our social group is intrigued to find out more and live it vicariously through him. As you can imagine it's something of a cultural minefield for a foreigner to date a local here and you'll need to work very hard to get the parents onside.

VISITING A BALINESE

One way or another you may end up being invited into a Balinese house and there are a fair few things worth knowing. Firstly you'll notice that in this island of beauty, everyone hides their houses away from the views by having walls around the house. It is, you may have guessed, to keep the demons out. As you enter the main door you'll immediately be confronted with yet another small wall. And it's there for the same reason. Demons can only go in straight lines and not round corners so this inner wall ensures they can't sneak through the door and into the compound.

Homes are made of several pavilions, usually raised off the ground just in case, well, the demons managed to get in anyway. There are three main elements to a household. There's the sacred space, the intermediary space and the impure part. (The bedrooms are in the intermediary space — get your minds out of the gutter.) The temple is positioned *kaja* (facing Mount Agung) and east (because the sun rises there). The kitchen faces *kelod* (to the sea) while bedrooms are positioned to the west but beds must be with the head facing Agung.

If all this sounds rather complicated then take this into consideration: The measurements in the house are all based on the head of the family's body measurements. The distance between elbow and thumb determines the thickness of the walls, while distances between elements of the house are determined by the size of his feet.

So much for the building you've entered but then it's all about the body. For the body, like the home, is a mini version of the cosmos. The head is the pure bit, the torso is neutral and below that is impure. Hence, you should take off your shoes when you enter a house, not just because they are

dirty from the roads but because they have been in contact with your feet.

Incidentally, this is why Balinese never build homes with more than one storey. Nobody wants to be in a room with feet above them. Incidentally to that incidentally, you'll notice that even the hotels here aren't high-rise monstrosities. That's because of a random decree that you can't build higher than the highest palm tree in the area. But I digress…

The main thing you need to know about the body is that below the waist is the impure part (for the feet and the stuff you were thinking about earlier with regard to the bedroom being in the impure part of the house). For this reason if you ever enter a Balinese temple you will be asked to wear a belt to separate the two sections of the body, the pure from the

A common sight in a deeply religious, ritualistic society: One of the Hindu gods within the pantheon of countless gods, displayed in a Balinese compound.

impure. It's not imperative to do this in someone's house, but it is respectful.

Somewhat surprisingly, there's no communal eating area in the home as people generally eat when and where they like. If you're lucky enough to be asked for dinner, don't be expecting cutlery. Generally, the Balinese hold the plate with the left hand and eat with the right. And do expect a lot of rice.

I did a quick straw poll of people to find out how many people had been invited into a Balinese compound, other than as part of a tourist trip. As expected, not many had and that goes to sum up what I said at the beginning of this chapter. But while my first reaction to this was sadness I now think it's not so bad. While I believe that the mixing of societies has to be a good thing, there's nothing innately wrong with everyone living in the way they want to as long as no group is negatively affecting the other. And that certainly seems to be the case here—that live and let live philosophy works both

It's a dog's life: There's always time for a book and a Bintang—even tourist dogs can get used to a more Hedonistic lifestyle!

ways. I don't know many expats who believe in Hinduism but equally I don't know any who disrespect it. Equally I don't know many Balinese who conform to the more hedonistic way of life we carry out, but they don't seem to judge us for it. All of which adds up to a place where everyone can live as they like and there is a healthy two-way respect—and that can be no bad thing.

Good form

When addressing Balinese people, much depends on the social situation. If you are in someone's house talking to an adult it is respectful to call a man Bapak (Pak for short) in Indonesian or Nene in Balinese. A female adult should be addressed as Ibu in either language. Elderly should be called Kaki and Dadong (Grandma and Grandad) in Balinese or Kakek and Nenek. For children, terms vary according to age. A generic term that you will often hear in restaurants and bars is either Mas or Mba, which is a catch-all term for one younger than you (male/female.)

In reality if you remember Pak and Ibu for adults of a similar or older age and Mas and Mba for those younger then you won't go far wrong.

Kylie Turner is a single female living in Bali and that makes her daily experience somewhat different from my own...

It's a strange (read: unnerving) feeling to walk around your new neighbourhood and be asked at every step: "Where you from?", "Where you going?", "What you doing?", "Where your husbaaaaand?", "Oh, why you not married?"

Coming from a Western culture where privacy is cherished and respected and strangers rarely look up from their iPhones walking down the street, let alone shout out a random hello to a stranger, this can be very confronting for a single female living on her own.

Depending on your mood, you can appreciate the novelty of people being friendly and wanting to meet you to being irritated at the privacy invasion. Their surprise at your single status acts as a constant reminder of your sad life as an unmarried, lonely thirty-something, living in Bali with a villa full of rescued street cats or Bali dogs. (That's not really my state of mind, but there are days when it feels like that and the probing does nothing to help.)

This game of 20 questions is just the locals' way of engaging with you, so once you realise you don't need to tell them your full life story and that the short and sweet (perhaps slightly fabricated) version will suffice, you enjoy these interactions much more. I find rehearsing my story is helpful and I have created the perfect 'husband' profile including his employment and physique (muscly, tall, tanned skin, works as an architect) for those awkward taxi drop-offs outside your villa when asked if you live alone, or where your husband is. In Bali the key to survival is to always be prepared—and don't forget your fake husband's name. [*Author's note*—said husband has occasionally been described as a tall, skinny author called Paul. It's easier to get your story straight if it's based on a real person.]

As well as the interrogators, there are the observers; the locals who don't say hello or shout out to you from their roadside perch, but instead clock your every move with a long stare as you innocently walk to the local minimart or corner store.

Learning a few basic greetings in Bahasa works a treat that surprises the watcher, starting with a big warm smile and "*Pagi! Apa kabar?*" which encourages a returned bright smile, generally a quick nod and the satisfaction they have observed you enough.

Visiting Bali on holidays is one thing; living here is an entirely different matter. My friends believe I am 'living the dream in tropical paradise, watching sunsets while drinking lychee martinis'... which is, admittedly, how I spend a large number of my weekends. However, it can also be tough navigating Bali's culture, people, and communication styles. Naturally there is a flipside of all of those ridiculously gorgeous, Instagram-worthy sunset photos.

The key to fitting in with locals is to speak some of the language, and Bahasa Indonesia is actually quite an easy language to learn, if you have time to practise it. The delight on the locals faces when they hear you utter a few clunky words more than makes up for all that time spent repeating the same words out loud in the privacy of your bedroom from the free language app you downloaded on your first day.

And it helps take their minds off wondering why you haven't got a husband, which is always a bonus.

[*Author's note* — as nice as the Balinese are there's no doubt there is a slightly seedy side to the place. While I don't get the attention Kylie does, I did once get home to my villa to find a man skulking around the end of my gang. He asked me for a light, which I proffered, and then he asked me if I wanted a blow job. I didn't hang around to find out whether he was offering a straight swap or he wanted something more than his cigarette lighting. I've had the same offer walking past one of the less salubrious salons as well, but funnily enough neither party seemed particularly bothered whether I had a wife or not.]

No offence

As you walk around Bali you will see many small baskets on the floor with flower petals, sweet food and perhaps a stick of burning incense. These are an essential part of the Balinese daily offerings to the gods. On temples you will find similar baskets. These are called *carang sari* (pronounced charang) They are sprinkled with holy water and are offerings to the gods.

As well as honouring the gods, the Balinese also satisfy the demons by placing offerings on the ground. These *segehans* are not as pretty and may contain rotten food (or, as I often observe, cigarettes) as the demons are not as discerning as the gods. These are placed on the floor and not on the temple. Both offerings are made in the morning and in the evening.

As you walk or drive around you may accidentally step on a *segehan* but don't worry if you do. For the Balinese, as long as the offering has been made, it is not important what happens afterwards so while avoiding them is still good manners, if you happen to kick one or crush one on your moped, don't worry that you have offended the locals.

CHAPTER 5

DIVING IN TO BALI LIFE

Bali is one of my favourite places in the world. In one of my past lives, I believe I was living on the island of Bali.

– Chip Conley

Bali life is very easy to slip into. Wearing flip-flops all day, every day, if wearing any footwear at all. Getting used to the permanent warm weather. Sunsets on the beach sipping an ice cold Bintang, or something a bit more tropical and potent. Generally getting used to a life that is a touch hectic in terms of the buzz but generally more laidback than that which you've probably come from. But before you get too settled into a life of tropical comfort there's some paperwork to deal with.

Sun and sea: The tropical climate of Bali demands flip-flops and an ice-cold Bintang every day.

BEING LEGAL—VISAS

Getting into Bali is a relatively easy process, but there's nothing simple about getting a visa for a long-term stay in Bali or Indonesia. When you first arrive you can pick up a tourist visa that involves a simple process at Immigration. This is now even simpler by virtue of the fact that Indonesia recently dispensed with the US$ 35 fee it used to charge; nearly every nationality is now exempt so you don't even need to worry about having cash on you or the extra queuing that used to be involved. The visa lasts for 30 days, extendable by another 30 days without too much fuss. At the other end of the spectrum there's the KITAS—the holy grail of expats living in Indonesia—that allows you to live and work in the country with the ability to come and go as you please. To get one you need to be employed by a business in Indonesia and the documentation required to get one is thorough.

All information is current at time of going to print. I recommend referring to baliexpatservices. com for updated information

The KITAS

Validity: up to 5 years; Initial stay: 1 year. Requirements:

- Diploma
- Reference Letter
- Valid passport
- Photo passport size
- Curriculum vitae
- Details and documents of company sponsor
- Company Sponsor documents:
- Copy of Article of association (Akta Pendirian Perusahaan)
- Copy of Company Business License (SIUP)
- Copy of Company Registration Number (TDP)
- Copy of Company Tax Identification Number (NPWP)
- Company Letter Head and Company Stamp
- Copy of Director ID card (KTP)

It'll set you back US$ 1,200 and then there's the fee incurred by the agency that organises it for you. You can try doing it yourself, but that way lies pain and misery. The good news is it's relatively straightforward to add a spouse and offspring; there's no extra charge from the government, although if your other half wants to work they won't be allowed.

The process itself is somewhat long and tortuous involving various embassy visits, forms and rigmarole but a good agent will take most of the pain out of it for you. Given enough preparation time you should be able to pick up your visa from the Indonesian embassy in your home country before you arrive. If not, then you might end up doing what I did—the infamous Singapore visa run.

If you don't have an Indonesian business willing to sponsor you there are interim options involving regular interaction with immigration and regular departures from the country to reactivate visas. There's the Social Culture Visa, which is every bit as ambiguous as it sounds. It's valid for six months with an initial stay of 60 days and monthly extensions are allowed four times. Requirements are:

The Social cultures Visa

- Sponsorship letter
- Copy of valid passport
- Photo passport size
- Copy of sponsor ID card (KTP)

Many visa agencies can act as the sponsor for a fee. Next up is the Business Visa—single or multi-entry—which is one step up. These last for a year, but again you have to leave the country every 60 days to fulfil the requirements and that gets a bit tiresome.

So much depends on what exactly you expect to be doing in Bali. If you want to open a business then the same agencies can work this through with you and it's a matter of patience as much as being allowed; that and the fact that any Indonesian business has to be sponsored by a local who theoretically has the right to pull the rug out from under you at any point as strictly speaking they 'own' the business. (For more information on opening a business see Chapter Nine.) But once you've done that then you can sponsor yourself to get a KITAS. I have one; many others live in the grey area in between.

If you're looking to retire to Bali it's relatively straightforward. As long as you have proof of retirement and proof that you have enough money to live on, Indonesia is happy to have you.

The Singapore run

Every day a bunch of expats do a day trip to Singapore to ratify their visas. This is my tale, as written at the airport awaiting my return flight:

I woke up this morning at 1:15 am—the kind of waking that comes soon after falling asleep when you know you've only got a small window for catching zzzs, you really can't afford to sleep through the alarm and you're paranoid you'll wake up late so instead you wake up early. I woke again at 3:30 am and sadly that was close enough to my alarm calls that I could cancel them all.

I had a quick shower and walked into the balmy night at 4:00 am, jumped on my scooter and finally discovered what Bali was like without traffic. Usually, transport to an airport is done via taxi but for my purposes today a scooter was fine and it also enabled me to find the world's cheapest airport parking at just US$ 1.50. To be fair, mopeds don't take up much space and it's mostly locals working at the airport that use that method of transport.

I had a nice prompt email from Air Asia a couple of weeks back saying my flight had been moved from 7:00 am to 6:20 am. Shame they never bothered to send the same one to the pilot as it was still scheduled for 7. Ah well, who needs sleep anyway? More annoying was that it would cut down my time at my destination and I needed all the time I could get. I was on a deadline.

I landed in Singapore, a city I had never previously visited and where I knew absolutely nobody. I jumped onto the local metro system and made for my destination: Orchard. Or was it? I had been so busy sorting out my house contract that I hadn't even looked this up. But this was what my mate had told me to do. Wasn't it? Self-doubt began to creep in. And while I had an hour to make my journey, I was cutting it mighty fine so there would be no second chances if I got to the wrong place. As I changed trains a girl started talking to me. "You were on the Bali flight, weren't you? Are you here to get your visa?" She was in the same boat (or train, I suppose) and was meeting the same person in the same hotel. Safety in numbers always helps.

We alighted at the stop that I knew then was the right one as her concurrence proved my brain hadn't been deceiving me. Asking people for directions to the actual meeting spot, we hurried as the clock was ticking for our 11:00 am deadline. We made the hotel at 11:00 am. But I had no idea who I was meeting. I had his name and his phone number if we could find a phone. Working on the assumption that he was probably here every day I figured the concierge must know him and so it transpired.

So, having found him, I did what you always do when you have just met a stranger for the first time in a foreign country. I gave him US$ 260, some passport photos, a telex and my passport. He thanked me, told me to come back at 4:00 pm and sent me out into Singapore to pass time. Sounds bonkers, but if you want a visa in these parts this is the game you play. Fortunately, he was in the same place at the allotted time and I did get my passport back with a nice big sticker in allowing me to live and work in Bali. That's well worth a 21-hour door-to-door journey. [I have heard a tale, possibly apocryphal, of someone who did a visa run and gave his passport to the wrong person and unsurprisingly never saw it again. Try explaining that one to your embassy.]

A LOAD OF BANKERS

If you have a KITAS, then banking in Indonesia is relatively straightforward. Simply choose a bank, go in, ask nicely with your relevant documents and they'll open up an account in the local currency and in various other international currencies to make moving cash from one place to the other a lot simpler. You have to sign a lot of bits of paper and you probably won't be sure what many of them are for, but it's not too difficult.

If you don't have a KITAS, things used to be more difficult but a recent relaxation of regulations has lessened the necessity for specific paperwork to open an account, meaning anyone should be able to open one without too much hassle. Some banks have already allowed for account opening with just a passport and now that should be even easier. Most banks have online banking and transferring money from a foreign currency account involves going into the branch and a bit of negotiating to get the best rate, but they're usually very good value. You'll get an ATM card and there's no shortage of machines on the island.

So far, so good.

But there are a few things to be aware of. The ATM card you get won't have your name on it. They literally pick a blank a card off a pile in a drawer, register it to your account and get you to allocate a PIN number to it. It works and can also theoretically be used in overseas ATMs; you can also use it for Point of Sale transactions just like your everyday bank debit or credit card. But it really does lack the power of your current bank's debit card and this is particularly key if you ever lose it and someone decides to go on a spending spree. Your usual recourse at this stage is to contact your bank and explain the situation; if they're content you didn't spend the money you'll get your cash back. That is very much NOT the case here. There's no consumer protection. What's more, as most outlets still predominantly request a signature as opposed to a PIN number it's far too simple for fraud to take place.

This is a reality that I was made harshly aware of after an evening that resulted in being relieved of my belongings. It was far too easy for my cards to be used and before I had reported anything there was around US$ 3,500 racked up on various cards. For my Australian bank and credit cards this was more of an inconvenience than a financial disaster as I was covered. But when it came to the Rp 10 million (US$ 750) on my Indonesian bank card, there was no such recourse.

As much as I love the Balinese people they tend to deal with any crisis by smiling, so when someone told me that my account had a much lower balance that it did the day before with a big grin on their face, my patience was tested. She pointed out that I would have been notified by phone whenever activity took place on my account, therefore

alerting me to any fraudulent activity, which is true. But then I retorted this doesn't help if you lose your phone and your card at the same time.

If that sounds annoying, it got a lot worse. I was told over the phone I wouldn't get my money back as it was my responsibility. I was told in my branch that I wouldn't get my money back because it was my responsibility. I accepted that fate and asked them very nicely if they would mind writing that down for me in a letter for my travel insurance company. And that's where the fun really started. When I say 'fun' I mean, of course, 'maddening, annoying, hair-pulling-out, illogical, crazy, unsympathetic nonsense'. I was told that couldn't be done and that the bank would have to open an investigation if I wanted a letter. Biting my tongue I patiently suggested that we open an investigation, which was done. The due date for response? Three and half months later. Needless to say I heard nothing in that time and when I went into the bank to query what was happening the same girl who started the whole thing disappeared, called head office in Jakarta and returned to tell me: "Yes sir, they have completed their investigation and you can't have your money back." My tongue has suffered serious damage in that place as I bit it again and pointed out that I was aware that was the case but that I just needed it in writing. 20 minutes of wrangling later I heard the immortal words "OK sir, we'll have to reopen the investigation…" I never got my letter.

I could also tell the story of when my relationship ended and the bank staff told us that we only needed one person to close our joint account. Once my partner had left Bali the same person declared that it was absolutely imperative that both of us were present, insisting there was no way to close the account unless she was there in person. Impasse was reached as I pointed out she wasn't coming back but that there must be a way to approach this. Two days later she miraculously found a form designed exactly for my situation, but that whole episode took up hours of my life and the same should not have to happen to you so I won't go into any more detail. Needless to say, my tongue took another hammering.

TAXING MATTERS

In theory, when you get a KITAS you need to apply for a tax number within six months. It seems reasonable enough and something that's relatively easily enforced, you would think. After all, when you go to renew your KITAS after a year they'll check up on that, won't they? Erm, no. In a classic case of 'not my department' there's no linkage so the Indonesian authorities (and I use that term to describe a disparate collection of unlinked entities) have no way of enforcing it. You go through hoops to get a visa to allow you work, filling in a million forms and paying money, but after all that they don't really check up on whether you're, you know, paying tax in the country you're working in.

In theory, part two: People resident in Indonesia pay tax on global earnings. So you declare everything you earn and pay tax accordingly. And the tax rates aren't unfair, between

5-30 per cent dependent on earnings (this in a country where many people are paid US$ 100 a month or less):

Tax Rates		
Tax Free	Up to Rp 36,000,000	0%
Band I	Up to Rp 50,000,000	5%
Band II	Rp 50,000,000 to Rp 250,000,000	15%
Band III	Rp 250,000,000 to Rp 500,000,000	25%
Band IV	Above Rp 500,000,000	30%

But in a country where many expats choose to live under the radar (i.e. without a KITAS), many simply don't pay tax at all. Indeed, if you don't have KITAS then I'm not even sure you can have a tax number so in a world where many people work online, you can't declare your earnings even if you want to. And the system here is not efficient enough to do anything about it. However, the new administration is beginning to put measures in place and inevitably they will get round to clamping down. Eventually someone is going to put a list of KITAS holders next to a list of tax numbers and work out the differences. When that might happen is anyone's guess, but if you're serious about living here, why risk being thrown out?

COMPLETELY UP FRONT
Bali property

Bali is not the easiest place to just dip your toe in the water if you're thinking of staying a few months to see whether you like it. The main reason for this is that the majority of properties available for rent have a minimum one-year lease and, here's the real kicker, that rent is payable up front. Indeed, many properties require an even longer commitment.

Monthly rentals are available but they tend to be small, studio apartment style places so if your vision of living in Bali, like mine when I first arrived, is a two-bedroom villa with a pool, then you need both cash and commitment.

You also need a dose of trust. Because while they do love paperwork over here that doesn't really seem to extend to rental contracts. Much of it seems to be done on a wing and a prayer. It is possible to get a *notaris* (notary) to draw up a legal contract but the majority of people don't bother. When I got my first villa I was expecting the estate agents to have a standard contract but I ended up writing parts of it myself and I'm convinced it wasn't worth the paper it was printed on. And even then there was one final sticking point between the landlord and I.

It was agreed that I would pay a 10% up front to secure the villa, followed by the balance of the year's rent within five days. He insisted that if I didn't pay the balance the deal was off and he would keep the deposit. Why he thought I might welch on the deal having already paid over a month's rent up front I still don't know. As you can imagine I wasn't prepared to risk my deposit if there was some sort of issue with my international bank transfer, so I wasn't prepared to agree. It was at this point the ridiculousness of our situation really hit me. He was concerned I wouldn't pay the rest of the balance for some reason and yet I was the one about to pay a year's rent to a man I had never met and so really it should be me worrying about him running off with the cash. And when I say cash, I mean cash. When the smallest note is worth around US$ 7.50, a year's rent involves a lot of paper but don't be surprised if that's what's asked for. Cash is very much still king here.

As it turned out he was a pretty good landlord and you need one, because if you pay a year's rent up front and you have a rubbish landlord then good luck getting anything fixed if it goes wrong. You do put yourself at their mercy to a certain extent. On the other side of that coin, once you've paid your rent you're pretty much free to do as you like. Where Western property owners might balk at letting you knock a nail in the wall, here pretty much anything goes. Want to build a wall? Install some windows? Change the furniture? The chances are you'll be allowed, as long as you're willing to pay for it.

One thing that I did agree to in my contract was the fact that twice a day for two minutes the locals were allowed access to the villa to put their offerings on the temple within our walls. This is occasionally disturbing as you can be sitting around minding your own business when a random stranger walks past the window. And yes, I did wake up on one of my first mornings, walk out to the pool without bothering to put any clothes on and smelt the incense in the air… only to realise the smell was so strong because there was a lady standing five metres away making an offering while I was standing naked, basking in the morning sun. Six months later they rebuilt our wall so access to the temple was on the outside not the inside, apparently because God doesn't like to look on naked flesh. I fear that horse had already bolted by then.

You can arrange to transport furniture from your old home, but depending on how long you're banking on staying it would be almost a shame to do that as Bali is a brilliant place to shop for furniture.

Our villa was furnished so we didn't need to stress about fitting it out, but again there is flexibility here; if you don't like the furniture that comes with the villa you can usually arrange to switch and if you find the perfect place but it happens to be unfurnished then you're in the right place. Unless you like IKEA (there's only one IKEA in Indonesia and it's just outside Jakarta). The great thing about furniture here is that it's almost all handmade in small stores so there's no mass-produced homogeneity. It also means you can easily get something bespoke relatively cheaply by talking to the relevant artisans.

Electricity in Bali is relatively straightforward as many villas work on prepaid systems whereby you pay up front, buying credit from stores just like you will for your mobile phone. It's available in so many places it's not a major drawback. There is a gradual move now to monthly post-paid bills but don't rely on that being the case. Power cuts are a feature of Bali life but in reality not overly prevalent. Writing this I can't actually remember the last one I had, so it must be getting more stable as they were fairly regular occurrences in my first year. Sockets are two-pin and my top tip if you're moving overseas with the various electric appliances that make their

way with you is to bring some four-way power boards so one adaptor can service a handful of devices.

Many of those devices you'll want to connect to the Internet, so that's your next step and the one thing I can say with surety is that by the time I have finished writing this sentence the situation will probably have changed. There are numerous Internet suppliers in Bali and the overwhelming impression seems to be that as soon as a service gets a good reputation it gets really popular and as a result speeds slow down because of the traffic on the network. There are fibre optic suppliers on the island now and if you are lucky enough that the cable is laid on your road then these are definitely the best options. Telekomsel's indiHome package includes high-speed Internet, TV and home phone for around US$ 30 a month. It's what I would have if I could and I would even pay them to lay the cable past my house if only they would only let me. If you can't get that then the best bet is not for me to reel off names here when the accuracy of the list will be instantly out-of-date. Talk to your neighbours and friends and see who has a good service. The good news is that Internet access here, while it is unstable, is improving all the time. [In the time it took to write this book I went through three different providers and ended up with a decent fibre optic connection—that kind of proves my point.]

While we're here we might as well cover mobile phones. As with most countries this is now incredibly straightforward. SIM cards are dirt cheap and prepaid *pulsa* (phone) and data is available on most street corners. You can also buy phones ranging from the very basic to the modern smartphones. Telekomsel is the major supplier and now boasts a 4G network.

So you've got walls (or not if you've chosen open-living), you're plugged in and you're hooked up. What next? Staff. If you want to do your own cleaning and washing then be my guest, but you'd be the only one I know in Bali who does. '*Pembantu*' means helper and pretty much everyone has one, whether full-time, daily or thrice-weekly. The price of labour here is very low so you can expect to find somebody to come six days a week, a couple of hours a day for around US$ 50-60 a month. Still want to do your own cleaning? Many homes will not have their own washing machines so the *pembantu* will deal with taking all your laundry, as well as cleaning and any other errands you'd like them to run, including replacing your water barrels. (If I hadn't mentioned it before the tap water is not suitable for drinking but the 19-litre bottles you're used to seeing in your office costs peanuts). Sometimes the *pembantu* comes with the house—so far I've been lucky with both of mine but some people not so much. There's nothing you can do about it if it's in your contract so just cross your fingers.

Washing machines are not the only thing missing from a

Balinese kitchen – you'll do well to find an oven; most kitchens boast only a couple of gas rings linked to a gas bottle. This is a reflection of the Balinese diet rather than the Western and it hardly makes for a chef's paradise. While you can buy various appliances to supplement your facilities depending on the size of the kitchen, it can be disappointing for those who love pottering in there.

As an aside — having an address in Bali is something of a luxury. My first villa literally did not have a number or a name. Trying to get a pizza delivered was a hassle. Receiving post wasn't worth even trying. To explain a little further, the road system here is made up of *jalans* (roads) and *gangs* (laneways). Very few villas are on a *jalan*, they tend to be down a *gang* and while the *gang* might have a name or a number.

that doesn't necessarily mean each building has a signifier. Alternatively, as with my present home, there are numbers for the four villas down my *gang* but the gang itself doesn't have a name so the numbers are related to the *jalan*. And while I live in 35D, next door is number 46. Confused? You will be. And the chances are, so will anyone trying to find your house.

And what of finding your own way around the island? Well, even in the modern world of Google Maps, it's not always straightforward. Much of the issue revolves around the fact that some streets have several different names. One of the main roads in Seminyak is called Jalan Kayu Aya and that's the name you'll find on Google Maps. But most people don't know that name and refer to it as a Jalan Oberoi because it culminates in the resort of the same name. It's also colloquially known as Eat Street because of the number of restaurants on it. Unsurprisingly, Google Maps doesn't cater for these varieties.

Then there's the accuracy of the maps in general. The story I heard was that the maps here were purchased form a third party and they simply don't have the accuracy you might find in the UK or Australia. According to the map there's a small gang next to my house that leads to the parallel road north of me; in reality it simply doesn't exist. Still, it's a hell of a lot easier with the map apps than it must have been without them. And it's quite nice to go back to directions as we used to have them... down that road, left at the landmark, end of the gang just past the 14th temple.

LEASE OF FAITH
Buying property in Bali
Trying to get your head round buying property in Indonesia is like trying to get a straight answer from a bank. As with

the banking system there has been some relaxation recently as the country seeks to encourage foreign investment but without giving away its lands.

One thing seems set in stone. Foreigners will not be allowed to 'own' land. And until recently the theory went that foreigners were not allowed to own property in Bali; in reality it was possible but there are lots of grey areas so I can't emphasise enough that getting up-to-date knowledge is vital.

Main ownership categories

There are three main ownership categories in Indonesia (with a bunch of variation such as the Right to Cultivate, but unless you're thinking of farming I'll ignore that as this is going to get complicated enough):

- The Right to Use (Hak Pakai)
- The Right to Build (Hak Guna Bangunan)
- The Right to Own (Hak Milik)

While foreigners couldn't have the latter two, they can take advantage of a Right to Use. Many expats wanting to invest in property here take a leasehold on a property which can be from 25 years to as long as 70 years. When a foreigner gets a Right to Use then the owners' Right to Own is temporarily transferred to them. This comes with an ability to sub-lease (rent out), making them an investment option.

The other option available is to have a sponsor — in the same way as we outlined when wanting to own a business here. This obviously involves having someone you trust but does offer the advantage that the property remains yours in perpetuity and isn't immediately reverted back to the owner at the end of a lease period.

In the early part of 2015 there was speculation that there was going to be a crackdown on what was perceived by authorities as illegal ownership of properties. By the end of the year this had come full circle with a government edict that decreed "Foreigners can own a house for a residence or investment with the right to use." So in theory the Right to Own was now available to foreigners. Understandably there is massive confusion and my tiny little brain has suffered just trying to get my head round the basics. In theory owning property in Bali could now get a lot easier. In reality just find a good estate agent who knows their stuff and if you have the will, there will be a way.

SHOPPING AROUND

Once I'd got past the first disastrous attempt at supermarket shopping recounted in Chapter One, I found it a lot easier to find the basics for stocking my home. But that isn't to say that it's all straightforward. As a random lady I bumped into in one supermarket despairingly said to me, "You can never get everything you need in one shop here." It was one of those moments when you raise your eyes at a complete stranger

Round in circles: I might not have worked it out straight away but there are plenty of places to buy food. Convenience stores are located at various points across the island.

and share the 'Bali look'. There are several big supermarkets in Bali that do pretty much cover everything you'll require, such as Carrefour on Jalan Sunset and the Hypermarket at Mal Bali Galeria, but they both involve a bit of a mission. Then there's a proliferation of medium-sized stores but just when you think you've found one that is well stocked, there will be something basic and obvious it doesn't have, which is what prompts random conversations with fellow expats you don't know halfway down the dried goods aisle.

It's actually quite nice to be in a place that has seasons (for growing, not weather). While it's kind of annoying when there are no strawberries, it's also a reminder that's the way things used to be at home before chemicals, science and mass importation got in the way to ensure there are always unnaturally bright red fruits available at your local supermarket. And yeah, it's annoying when you buy some and a few of them have gone off, but also it's a reminder that it's all a bit more real.

Inevitably there are things you can't get. Good quality meat can be hard to find (good quality bacon especially—sob), Australians can't find their beloved Vegemite at every turn while really good chocolate is my must-have import from trips abroad. Whenever I travel abroad for work there are always wish lists of things my mates want me to bring back; one of my good friends asked me to bring Super Noodles back from the UK on one trip which seemed to me a little like bringing ice to someone who lived in Antarctica, but we all have our home comforts.

At this point I am contractually obliged by one of my favourite people to mention tampons. Painful experience has taught me that hell hath no fury like a woman without access to them and they're not widely available here so it pays to stock up as and when you can. I noticed that the alcohol delivery service Warung on Wheels now has them as a delivery option which might help, but best be prepared.

Away from the supermarket, shopping for fruit and vegetables at the markets is much cheaper, a more fun experience and supports the locals, although much depends on the strictness of your health and safety morals. I'd certainly balk at the fish and meat for that reason alone. I'm no health and safety freak, but a bit of refrigeration never did any of those products any harm.

When it comes to shopping for clothes as opposed to food, Bali is somewhat dichotomous. On the one hand there's the flea markets and proliferation of stalls trading mainly in knock-off Aussie Rules, basketball or football shirts. Fake shoes are a huge seller, while knock-off electrical goods also have a big high street presence. Haggling is pretty much obligatory and trademark infringement is guaranteed.

> One object for sale at nearly all of these stores that has bemused me since the moment I first saw them is the wooden phallus. These come in all manner of sizes and painted colours. Some even hand a bottle opened to give that practical element. There are no T-shirts saying "My girlfriend went to Bali and all I got was a wooden penis" but there are loads with such inspiring slogans as "I'm not gay but $20 is $20."

But rubbing shoulders with these fairly insalubrious 'emporiums' is a fairly high-end shopping experience. Some top name brands have penetrated the market with surf shops such as Billabong and Quicksilver (obvious given the surfing link), Havaianas, Nike and Oakley. Kuta has the Beachwalk Shopping Mall with even more Western brands, including Zara and Topshop. But more intriguing and enjoyable are the local clothing brands that have made a name for themselves offering quality design. But if you're coming to Bali thinking you'll pick up quality clothes on the cheap you might be disappointed. Because these stores are aimed at tourists the prices are not too dissimilar to that you might find at home and the quality is not guaranteed. It does make a nice change from the humdrum of high street shopping in the West though. And there are loads of tailors and manufacturers around if you want to get things copied.

DRIVING FORCE
Getting around

Getting fruity: There really isn't much the Balinese can't transport by moped.

The vast majority of people in Bali get around by scooter or moped and that includes expats. It's a much simpler and faster way of getting from A to B, if a tad more dangerous. Hiring a scooter is incredibly simple; probably too simple. The chances of anyone bothering to ask for a driving licence or even a passport are very slim so anyone can jump on one with a minimum of fuss. On the one hand this makes it very easy to arrange, on the other you know that the roads are full of people who might not even know how to drive. Assuming you're staying long-term, many agencies do monthly rentals in the region of Rp 700,000 (US$ 50).

But just because you don't need a licence to rent a bike doesn't mean you don't need a licence to ride one. To be a legal moped driver in Bali you should have an International or Indonesian Driving Licence. To get one of the latter you need to go to a specific police station (Poltabes in Jalan Gunung Sanghyang in West Denpasar) with a copy of your passport, including your visa stamp and your home country

Heavy traffic: The days of muddy tracks, bicycles and carts are well behind Bali.

driving licence (not necessarily moped-specific). To get a licence for one month of a tourist visa costs Rp 375,000 and the price is pretty much the same for however long your visa lasts, so if you have a KITAS you'll pay the same for a year. It can be a drawn-out process at the police station, but they're always on the lookout for a bule to make a few quid from. I've renewed mine twice; on the first occasion they put the price through as a local and on the second the office was closed but they magically opened it just for me. On both occasions I'm pretty sure that most of the money went in the pocket of the officer concerned but it got me in and out quickly so I didn't really care.

So what happens if you haven't got a licence? Well, there are two ramifications: if you are stopped by the police and do not have one you can expect to pay a fine (whether official or more of the bribe variety). But an even bigger ramification is that many insurance policies do not cover you for moped/

motorbike unless you have a local licence—and you don't really want to be riding these things uninsured. Another thing you can get fined for is not wearing a helmet—theoretically it's illegal, realistically it's rarely enforced. You'll see a lot of people riding around without them, but not me. I may not be the world's best looking man, nor its most intelligent, but what little I do have in the ways of looks and brains I am quite keen to keep hold of. And don't get me started on people who have their kids on mopeds without helmets. If you want to take the chance be my guest; inflicting that chance on a kid is criminal in my opinion.

If you do want to take the car option then again it's relatively simple to hire one and the process to get a driving licence is very similar to that for a scooter, but labour costs are low enough here that you might prefer to just hire a driver anyway to take the strain of getting through the traffic.

There's little in the way of public transport here and the taxis are hit and miss to say the least. Bluebird Taxis are the most reputable and their drivers can always be relied on to put their meter on straight away. Elsewhere it can be pot luck but identifying a Bluebird taxi isn't always easy— the more unreliable taxis are painted similar colours with similar logos so picking a legit cab can be something of an acquired art form. Some will put the meter on when you insist, others will just demand a fare way in excess of what you should be paying. The actual price still isn't particularly expensive, but it's a principle thing and you know it's based on the fact that for every expat that says no there's a tourist who won't. If you're anything like me, and the majority of my friends to be fair, you'll argue massively over a couple of dollars and when friends come to visit they'll wonder why you get so angry about it.

Uber is available in Bali although there has been a big backlash from local taxi drivers and signs abound saying 'No Uber'. Getting one from the airport involves covert communication lest the driver incur the wrath (which can involve violence) of the established cabbies. GrabTaxi is a similar service around here yet has had a similar welcome, while Go-Jek is a great alternative for short journeys with no luggage—think Uber but on a moped instead of in a car. (Go-Jek actually goes way beyond just getting you from A to B, you can use them as couriers, get them to do your shopping and, just checking my app, they can even send someone round to your house for a Go-Massage. I'll be back in an hour...)

Learning to ride a scooter—a blog post

"An Australian dies every nine days in Bali." That was the single most-repeated statistic thrown my way before I embarked on this little chapter of life. Inevitably, I pointed out that as I am not Australian the statistic was irrelevant, but as one of the big dangers here is riding a scooter it's worth a line or two on what riding a moped is like in these parts.

Bloody mental, that's what it's like. But while my first few days getting amongst the seemingly insane, chaotic traffic led me to believe I would never get used to it, now I really quite enjoy it as a way of getting around. It's amazing how quick you get used to what at first appears a completely anarchic road system.

You need to get used to traffic lights. Before they go green, everyone waiting for them to go green will beep their horn, just on the off-chance that you haven't realised they're about to go green (which you can usually work out as they have countdown clocks). But just because the beeping has started and just because the light has gone green doesn't mean it's necessarily time to twist the throttle, because first you have to wait a few seconds for the people going the other way to finish treating the red light as though it was actually just a different shade of green. As one local put it to me—in Australia an amber light means traffic slows down, in Bali it means speed up as everyone hurries to rush through.

Now traffic can be hideous, especially around Seminyak, and while being on a scooter allows you to weave around traffic you can still get clogged up. Which is where it becomes important to realise that pavements may nominally be footpaths, but if you're in a hurry and the traffic's not moving then they're also fair game for buzzing along to make some progress. Obviously the idea is not to do that when people are walking down them (although that doesn't stop a lot of locals doing so, leading to the odd Mexican stand-off), but otherwise crack on. Talking of pedestrians, there are zebra crossings but these are ostensibly just bits of paint on the road for all the effect they have. Watching newbies stand there expecting the traffic to stop is quite amusing—it ain't gonna happen for them.

It might appear then, that there are no real rules, but there is one incontrovertible law of the road that everyone sticks to; the one that everyone lives by and no one ever breaks. And that rule is, it's everyone for him or herself. But that's not quite as crazy as it sounds as more often than not it works out quite well. The unwritten rule seems to be 'I'll make sure I don't hit you as long as you make sure you don't hit me'.

Confidence is the most important driving skill around these parts, although judgement of distance comes a pretty close second. Having the nous not to drive when you're pissed and to wear a proper helmet is also quite a handy characteristic. Of those Australians that die every nine days I would love to see some statistics on how many die because of a motorbike accident, how many of those wore helmets and how many of those were drunk. [Author's note—during the writing of this book I read a headline that is peak Bali: "A 16-year-old Australian has died in the basement of a Kuta Hotel where he was illegally driving a motorcycle." You couldn't make that up.] Now I'll hold my hand up—I have done the odd short journey in Seminyak on the back of someone else's bike without a helmet. But 99.5 per cent of the time I use one and not just the shoddy thing that came with the scooter I have rented, but a proper full-face helmet.

They say there are two types of people who ride scooters in Bali: those who have had an accident and those who will have an accident. I'm hoping to buck that trend but I'm realistic enough to try to minimise the ramifications if I don't.

CLASS ACT
Finding a school

There is a range of international schools on offer for parents in Bali. The Canggu Community School is very popular with Western expats, not least because of its location. Canggu is one of the island's biggest expat communities and the CCS is located almost adjacent to the Canggu Club of which most families are members; it has excellent sports facilities. The school and club are very much epicentres of the family communities around here. Another alternative in this part of the world is the Australian International School and Montessori is also an option. Meanwhile, over in Sanur, another popular expat hangout, the Bali International School is a favourite.

Prices vary—a quick glance at the Canggu Community School fees for 2016-17 suggest that for pre-schoolers, annual bills will total around Rp 120 million (US$ 9,000) and it only gets more expensive as the kids get older.

The most remarkable school in these parts is close to Ubud. The Green School was awarded the 2012 Greenest School on Earth by the US Green Building Council and it's easy to see why. It is built entirely out of bamboo and the 'heart of the school' is believed to be the biggest freestanding bamboo building in the world; it's stunning. But while the use of bamboo is an essential part of the school's green credentials, it is only the beginning of the story.

Most schools don't have cows. This one does and they play a vital part in the composting programme. All the leftover food (and banana leaves used to serve it on) is composted, helped out by a couple of cows who like to munch their way through some of the leftovers before, shall we say, depositing it back whence it came in a slightly different form.

This accelerates the composting program and said compost is then used by the children to grow vegetables. They are served for lunch and so the circle starts again.

The vortex is a school project unlike any I ever did. Water from the river flows into the vortex, creating a whirlpool effect turning a turbine that creates energy. A combination of solar panels and this vortex create more energy than the school uses. Once the water has left the vortex it runs through a filter that picks out all the litter before continuing its journey downriver.

It's a school with an environmental focus, but it also approaches education in a different way from the norm, encouraging project-based learning rather than mere classroom indoctrination. International students make up a large part of the group but the local scholarship programme dramatically increases the number of local students who are able to attend, adding to a United Nations of pupils.

Lessons in schooling

Nicole Rajkovic moved to Bali in 2015 with partner Joar and three-year-old daughter Annika, and took time to find the right level of education:

Schools are something of a mixed bag here. There weren't a lot of options when it came to day care when we first arrived, but in the last 12 months around a dozen new centres have opened up, offering a range in style and price of education and stimulation for under-5s.

One thing to realise is that there isn't much in the way of long day care; most services end around 2.30 pm, although there are a handful that do open till 5.30 pm. Our little one took a little while to settle in at the first place that was conveniently located a few minutes' walk from where our place was.

However, we found the carers, who did not speak English, were not willing to speak in Bahasa Indonesian to our daughter as she did not understand. This didn't overly concern us or her, but we did try to change it and despite several visits to the head carer it continued. Add on to that the fact they had no books in English and also refused to read to her in Bahasa Indonesian.

We moved to Indonesia and as this is the national language so why this wasn't taught was of confusion to us. We tried a second centre and encountered a similar issue; however all carers were bilingual here and simply spoke in English to the children, so at least there was communication.

Most staff are carers, not educators at pre-school centres in Bali. There may be one trained person in the entire centre, not always in each classroom as you may expect. Safety standards are extremely different from what you're probably used to and there is no official notification of injury or such that is required.

The trick to moving here generally is not coming in with rose-tinted glasses; it's critical to avoiding a massive shock. Remember you're not on holiday and it's not always going to be paradise island, but it mostly is if you tread warily and do your due diligence where required.

A HEALTHY ATTITUDE
Health insurance and hospitals

While Bali will probably never win awards for the quality of its healthcare, it isn't quite the medical backwater that many fear. The Balinese have a, shall we say, different approach to medicine related to their religion and many might give hospitals the swerve. But for those of us who are keen on such facilities there are some good ones around. I've had to take various friends and attended hospital myself and the one I use (Siloam) is clean, efficient and inspires confidence.

A caveat to that is that my visits have only been for minor issues; I've also known people who have had to travel to Singapore or Bangkok for more serious conditions. So on the one hand you can be confident that basic healthcare is covered and covered well; on the other you need to be prepared to travel for serious treatment.

Whether you are treated in Bali or not it's going to cost you money, so being insured is a no-brainer. As a Westerner used to having healthcare in the country I reside in, my first instinct was to look for a local provider and this proved somewhat problematic. I could make neither head nor tail of what was and wasn't covered by the policies I looked at and it's safe to say the customer service wasn't quite up to the standard I was hoping for. Apparently there are a couple of providers that offer reasonable options but, and it's a very big but, if you're going to end up needing to fly to another country for treatment then local health insurance isn't going to actually cover everything you need. Here's the reality: going to hospital for something minor is one thing; for something serious you'll want to be covered for expatriation so you can be flown home to the place you want to be treated at. A local policy isn't going to provide that.

My solution was to get travel insurance. Not only was this clear in terms of what was and wasn't covered, it had the benefit of also covering my belongings. I did come a cropper, however, by taking a single trip policy and didn't realise that the second I stepped foot back on Australian soil the policy became null and void. It took some research to find a better option but it is feasible and certain companies do specialise in expat insurance.

The chances are you're going to spend a lot of time outside when you're in Bali. Why wouldn't you? The climate is made for it and that climate is probably one of the reasons you came here. As I've already mentioned, outdoor living is a fairly standard thing here and generally a villa will have closed bedrooms with aircon, but very often open living areas with drop down 'curtains' for use during rainy season in place of walls. My friends in the UK find it hard to get their head round the idea that I have neither doors nor proper walls to my living area. And if the idea takes some getting used to, the reality of living like that can as well.

My biggest issue with it at the moment is the squirrels that steal my bananas. I tried keeping them in ziplock bags (the bananas. not the squirrels), but to no avail. I said earlier on in this book that burglary isn't much of a thing in these parts but that evidently doesn't extend to the animal kingdom. And it's not just squirrels that have access to your home. Mosquitoes are the biggest pest and they're something of a fact of life, especially if you have a pool and even more so during rainy season. My current abode is situated in a tropical garden, which is an amazing place to be, but you have to put up with the various buzzy things that it attracts.

And there's the climate, which can be uncomfortably hot sometimes as opposed to opulently amazing. But the reality is you have a choice here—there's always the air-conditioned refuge if you need it and some do choose to close off their open living area. But for me it's everything living in the tropics is about and the odd bite or missing banana is a small price to pay for that luxury.

Grease my palm

Corruption is a thing in Bali, there's no getting away from that fact. It's easy to be contemptuous and dismissive of it, but that would be somewhat simplistic. At the basic level it's the 'fines' we've already mentioned for not having a driving licence or not wearing a helmet. Often this boils down to the police officer in question wanting some lunch money. I remember getting pulled over by one gent in uniform who insisted he was only checking my documents for my safety, but I knew he was gutted the moment I pulled out my Indonesian driving licence.

Not that I have not ever paid the bribe. After all, that driving licence is the one I, erm, happily paid extra to get done quickly.

A friend of mine from the UK very kindly brought over rather more than the prescribed limit of duty free alcohol on one visit. The customs chap pointed out that his extra bottles should be destroyed but a quick conversation and a few dollars in the back pocket saw him safely through.

When you're talking minor offences a few Rupiah here and there talks. But it reaches up the chain. One case that hit the news revolved around a bucks (stag) night where the revellers ended up with an AUD 25,000 bribe for hiring strippers. A huge backlash ensued and the police officers found themselves in a spot of bother.

There's a lot of hypocrisy around corruption. If you're going to ride around Bali without a driving licence but complain about corruption when someone pulls you over and sticks some cash in their pocket, consider what would happen if you did the same in your home country. There'd be no getting out of it for a few dollars for a bloke who earns a couple of hundred dollars a month to have some lunch.

CHAPTER 6

SELAMAT MAKAN

'Dishes full of intensity, beautiful flavours and a philosophy and technique that made us want to run to the kitchen and fire up the pan.'

— uncorneredmarket.com

Bali has evolved into a foodies' paradise. Long gone are the days remembered not so fondly by Bali veterans who faced limited options when it came to going out for a meal. Now expats and tourists alike are spoilt for choice with a cornucopia of culinary offerings covering everything your appetite desires.

It's not just the explosion of the restaurant scene here that makes it so attractive for those who have a love of food, however, because Balinese and Indonesian cuisine has a lot going for it. And that means you can keep it real with the locals and indulge in a mouthwatering range of street food highlighting the traditional dishes that still tantalise and satisfy the locals, or hit one of the island's many high-class restaurants showcasing cuisine from all over the globe. If that's not enough to get your tastebuds tingling then you need to factor in a range of stunning settings showcasing interior design of the highest quality or a design that cannot be replicated by man—natural scenery that will take your breath away.

The Balinese themselves keep things simple with a diet based around rice—for all the fields growing the stuff around the island there's still a requirement for the island to import the stuff to satisfy the demand. The majority of locals will eat the stuff three times a day but it's something of a shame for them because while the staple local dishes are based on it they have a lot more in their locker. The Balinese are not averse to eating out; you'll often see the locals chowing down at roadside eateries or even enjoying the local version of fast food, which is why you see so many local *warungs* by the roadside.

GOING LOCAL

Warung is a key word in these parts—its specific definition relates to a part of the family compound that is public facing and used to generate income, so it could be a small store selling goods. But in reality it has become synonymous with small eateries and as you walk around these parts you'll see them on every street. They're fundamentally basic

affairs with limited menus and table settings where locals congregate to chew the fat and chew the local fare. You'll find uncomplicated classics such as *nasi* goreng (fried rice), *nasi campur* (mixed rice) or *sote ayam* (chicken noodle soup) sold here, cooked on basic facilities. Elsewhere you'll find vendors on street corners, with portable barbecues used to cook one of the island and the country's quintessential specialities—*sate* (satay).

And if you think that's accessible food then you ain't seen nothing yet because a lot of food offerings are more mobile. The term fast food takes on a whole new meaning when the food is stored and cooked on the back of a moped, which is often the case with the corn sellers. The local *bakso* soup comes a little more sedately as it's created in handpulled carts that set up wherever business offers itself. A bell announces its arrival just like ice cream vans in the west. *Bakso* consists of the meatballs from which the name derives mixed with broth, noodles and vegetables. I'll be honest, it's not my cup of tea—or soup—but the locals can't get enough.

Meals on wheels: Some *warungs* don't involve you having to move at all.

More up my alley is *babi guling* — suckling pig. Ask anyone in Bali and they will all have their favourite purveyor of this local classic, but the best I ever had wasn't even in a restaurant. Sitting at a bar on the beach in Kuta one evening the owner asked our group if we fancied suckling pig the following night. For around US$35 they pre-cooked it and delivered the entire pig to our table on the beach...

It was so big we fed half the people on the beach with it while the sand was still lodged in our toes.

DO IT YOURSELF

If you're really fascinated by Balinese food and you want to learn more about it then you're in luck. Doing a Balinese cooking course is a great way to find out more about the island's culinary history, learn some of the techniques that have been passed down through history and, of course, taste the results of your day's labours. Many courses take place in hotels or restaurants but to me this loses some of the authenticity that this kind of experience demands. There are classes that involve going out to market to learn more about the ingredients and purchase the vital elements of the day with the cooking then taking place in family compounds. This becomes more of an immersive Balinese experience rather than merely a cooking class.

Rae Richards (see page 116 for her story) lived in Bali for six months and got seduced by the flavours of Balinese cuisine. She discovered that Balinese cuisine uses an incredible variety of spices that create complex flavours when blended with vegetables, meat and fish. It shares many of Indonesia's national dishes such as *nasi goreng*, *gado gado* and *sate* (satay) but often with a local twist. As an example, Balinese *sate* sticks are traditionally made with chicken that is minced rather than cubed. Another key difference is that most of Bali's population is Hindu as opposed to the Muslim majority throughout the rest of Indonesia. So beef isn't on the day's menu —albeit beef *rending* is a hugely popular dish in these parts— but *babi guling* (spit roasted suckling pig) is a huge favourite.

Bali also has its own specialities influenced by other Asian cuisines, including Chinese and Indian, and also exhibits hints of Dutch, Spanish and Middle Eastern cuisines. The famous peanut sauce would never have existed if peanuts weren't introduced from Mexico by Portuguese and Spanish merchants in the 16th century.

Most of the common Balinese dishes are named according to their main ingredient and a description such as the cooking method. The Indonesian favourite of *nasi goreng* is nasi (rice) and *goreng* (frying). *Nasi campur* (*campur* meaning 'mixed') is a Balinese speciality with a scoop of white rice and small portions of a number of other dishes that may include curry, *lawar*, *babi guling*, *sate*, vegetables, tempeh or eggs with sambal.

Many of the distinctive flavours come from the spices that are used. When talking about particular dishes or sauces you may hear of '*bumbu*', which is the Indonesian word for a spice mixture or seasoning. Nutmeg, clove, *galangal* (aromatic ginger) and pandan leaves are all native to Indonesia but many of the other spices that are now at the core of Balinese cuisine were introduced from mainland Asia in ancient times, including black pepper, turmeric, shallot, garlic, ginger, cinnamon, candlenut, coriander and tamarind.

Coconuts are an essential ingredient in Balinese life. Coconut milk and sometimes young coconut flesh are used as ingredients in many sweet and savoury dishes. Coconut oil is extracted from the kernel of matured coconuts and also used for cooking while the husks are dried and burnt as charcoal, giving *sate* its distinctive smoky flavour. The local palm beer is made from gum extracted from the tree's flower buds. Coconut palm leaves are used to wrap food or to make offerings to the gods and the timber from the tree trunk is a popular building material. As if all that wasn't enough, palm (coconut) sugar is made by tapping the sap of the tree and boiling it down to produce a syrup that is then crystallised into the solid lump that you may have used in Asian recipes.

While it's fascinating to read about, it's much more fun to consume and even more so to learn the trade secrets that have evolved over hundreds of years.

Rae's Balinese Food Adventure

Rae took time out to go on a Balinese food adventure and this is what she learned:

My day started with a trip to Ubud market where we watched the ladies making the colourful '*canang sari*' and '*segehan*' temple offerings that you see almost everywhere you go on the island. Surrounded by huge wicker baskets filled with flowers, it's mesmerising to watch as they skilfully weave palm leaves into the small baskets that hold the offerings to the gods. Every market has its own temple where the sellers go each morning to make an offering in the hope of a good day's trade.

At one of the fruit stalls inside the market, our guide tells us about the fruits that are native to Bali, including banana, snake fruit, jackfruit, durian and mangosteen (known in Bali as the 'Queen of the fruit') and seven different types of mango. He buys a few pieces of each and hands them around for us all to have a taste.

We pop in to the spice vendor with his huge array of dried spices and a vegetable stall selling everything from fragrant limes smaller than a golf ball to long beans, so named because they can be over a metre long. Next stop is a stand of kitchen tools where we learn that in Bali, everyday food is prepared by women using the smaller knives

they also use to make the temple offerings. Ceremonial food is usually prepared by the men using a larger cleaver-style chopping knife. The backbone of every Balinese kitchen is the dish-shaped stone mortar and right-angle pestle (*cobek* and *ulek ulek*) that is used for grinding spices as well as making *sambal* and peanut sauce.

You can't talk about Balinese food without talking about rice; about 70 per cent of Bali's population farms the stuff and the paddy fields and terraces are popular tourist attractions as well as places for producing the island's staple food. The word *nasi* (rice) also means 'meal,' which is no surprise when you consider that most Balinese eat rice for breakfast, lunch and dinner.

The majority of rice grown in Bali is white rice, but they also grow red and black varieties that are typically used in desserts. Most rice is grown on family plots and used just to feed the family, which seems excessive until you do the maths. The average person consumes about half a kilogram (1.1 lbs) of rice per day, so a family compound of 20 people will go through 10 kg (22 lbs) of rice in a single day, or 3.65 tonnes (8,046.9 lbs) per year.

When the time came to stop listening and start doing I was faced with a gamut of fresh organic ingredients that were laid out waiting for us, including a rainbow array of vegetables as well as fresh turmeric and *galangal*, chillies and peanuts. Then it was down to business as we washed our hands for the first of many times (I was pleased to see they're serious about food hygiene) and got to our stations to start preparing the ingredients for the day. Some of the men on my course were allocated to the 'Balinese blender', a large mortar and pestle like we'd seen at the market, to start grinding the peanuts and spices into a paste for the peanut sauce.

One thing we quickly realised is that it's all about the yellow sauce. *Bumbu kuning*, or basic yellow sauce, isn't a dish in itself but we used it as a key ingredient in four of the other recipes. It's fun to make because you get to use a *lu* and *lesung* to grind the ingredients into a paste. A *lu* is a long hand-held wooden pole used to grind the spices in the *lesung*, a large stone bowl that's placed on the ground. Sadly it's not something I have at home, but a food processor will do the job just as well.

Once all the dishes were done and our *sate* skewers had been expertly grilled over coconut charcoal, one of the transformer workbenches then became a presentation table where our culinary creations were beautifully laid out as a long buffet. All that cooking was hungry work so our first plateful was gone within moments.

No feast is complete without dessert, so next up was *kolak pisang* that is cooked by simmering slices of banana in coconut cream with palm sugar syrup.

My favourite dish of the day would be the tempe *kering* (fried tempeh),

which just goes to show that you can make anything taste good if you deep fry it in coconut oil and add heaps of sweet soy sauce.

With an entrée involving fascinating visits to the markets and rice fields, followed by a main course of getting to know the ingredients and cooking techniques and a dessert of getting to consume what we had created, the cooking school has the perfect menu for anyone with an interest in cooking. Add locals and their knowledge as a permanent garnish and here you have all the ingredients for a fantastic day out.

What's cooking?

Fancy a cooking course? Want to know what you'll be making? Check out this tasty list from Rae's day in the kitchen:

- *Sup Jamur*—Clear mushroom & vegetable soup
- *Bumbu Kuning*—Basic yellow sauce
- *Kare Ayam*—Chicken in coconut curry
- *Sate Lilit Ayam*—Minced chicken grilled on bamboo sticks
- *Gado Gado*—Vegetables in peanut sauce
- *Jukut Urab*—Coconut and snake bean salad
- *Pepes Ikan*—Steamed fish in banana leaves
- *Tempe Kering*—Deep fried tempeh in sweet soy sauce
- *Nasi Goreng Ayam*—Fried rice with chicken
- *Kolak Pisang*—Boiled banana in palm sugar syrup

A class above: Host Puspa shows off the array of food made in her kitchen—see 'What's cooking?' on the left for the complete list.

GOING UPMARKET

There's no doubting then that Balinese food is varied, tasty, intriguing and enjoyable. And it's not just Bali that has a great culinary heritage—once you've started exploring you'll find many of the islands in Indonesia have similarly enjoyable food with some similarities but also unique specialities. But I mentioned that Bali is a foodies' paradise not just because of the local dishes but the awesome array of high-end restaurants of which there are far too many to even keep count of.

While the *babi guling* on the beach goes down as one of my favourite meals in my time on the island—as much for the experience as the quality of the food—I'm really spoilt for choice when it comes to classy eating establishments. They are so numerous that when my friends turn up with a list of the ones they want to go to, they usually leave without getting anywhere near ticking off everything on it. I could fill up much of this book with listings and while it's possible to go 'round the world in 80 restaurants' within Bali I've whittled it down to 10% of that. And even then I've left out some of my favourites. So here's how to go round the world in eight restaurants without leaving Bali.

- **Merah Putih — Indonesia** (www.merahputihbali.com) My perennial favourite and the one place I insist on taking everyone that visits. The space itself is stunning, capacious and it grows on me a little more each time I eat there. The canvas columns are not just visually impressive but have a practical use as they harvest the rainwater that funnels down the inside of them. The food is a combination of traditional and modern Indonesian dishes and while the menu continually evolves, the delicious essence never changes. To further explore Indonesian cuisine, **The Warung** (www.alilahotels.com/uluwatu/dining) has an in-depth menu that allows you to go on a culinary tour of Indonesia with specialities from various islands.
- **Sardine — Mediterranean** (www.sardinebali.com) It's not the only restaurant to utilise rice fields as a backdrop but few do it better; its interior design ethos extends the open-air bamboo construction with its dramatic high ceilings throughout the working farmland. The paddy field backdrop is beautifully lit and a pre-dinner cocktail in its environs is the perfect way to begin any meal experience. The seafood is sourced locally every morning in Jimbaran and complemented by vegetables, herbs and salads from the restaurant's organic farm in the mountain village of Bedugul. It's a breezy, open-air food theatre that walks that fine line between complete relaxation and refined class.

- **Sarong—Asia** (www.sarongbali.com)
  The menu offers a tantalising array of Asian offerings taking inspiration from the chef's extensive forays into Asia, with particular influence from street food styles. The restaurant calls it Cuisine Culture. Sarong is a well-established favourite among the Seminyak crowd looking for a refined dining experience. Everything about it screams elegance (actually it's more likely to whisper it than scream) and somehow they've created a restaurant that can host a large crowd and yet make you feel as though your table is in its own little bubble. The décor looks as though it has been taken from a Victorian drawing room. It looks as though it shouldn't really be practical for dining, yet when it comes to the crunch it's absolute perfection. It would be remiss not to mention its sister restaurant, **Mama San** (mamasanbali.com), another perennial island favourite.

- **Metis—France** (www.metisbali.com)
  Metis one of the first names on the lips of many
  a visiting gastronome and while its attraction
  is undimmed, it has undergone something of a
  transformation since 2015. Gone is the rice field that
  used to be an integral part of the restaurant, to be
  replaced by Le Jardin, a perfectly manicured garden.
  This change came on the back of a new bar and lounge
  area that saw the restaurant's construction take over
  more of the land. But this institution, with its grandiose
  gallery and impressive fascia, still retains the essence
  of what made it so popular in the first place—with the
  standalone foie gras menu as indicative of what you'll
  get here as anything I could describe individually.
- **CasCades—Western / Eastern fusion**
  (www.cascadesbali.com)
  If we're trying to go round the world in eight restaurants,
  CasCades does it in one, sourcing Australian wagyu
  beef, Canadian lobster and French *fois gras*. Executive
  chef Nic Vanderbeeken combines Western dishes with
  Asian flavours and the place is forever winning awards.
  It also hosts regular special events showcasing some of
  the world's finest chefs, but while the food is exquisite
  there is more to this place than just the victuals. The
  setting is classic Ubud as the Viceroy Bali resort in
  which it resides is in the Valley of the Kings, a tropical
  rainforest setting that will make this a meal to remember
  before you've bothered to even taste anything.
- **Barbacoa—Latin America** (www.barbacoabali.com)
  I like the chapa bread at this place so much I could eat
  that alone and still be happy. It comes with a sauce
  made up of balsamic, olive oil, chilli and garlic cloves

roasted 24 hours previously and I can't get enough of it. But I have to because I'm a meat lover and whether it's the 8-Hour Wood Fired Asado of the Day that you (well I, anyway) simply can't ignore or the chorizo that comes with a choice of chimmichurri or red pepper jam there's a lot to leave room for. In its own words, Barbacoa "is dedicated to BBQ, wood fire, charcoal and loads of smoke" and while that may not be everyone's choice, it's certainly one of mine.

- **Ju-Ma-Na—French fine dining with a Japanese influence** (www.banyantree.com/en/ap-indonesia-ungasan-bali/ju-ma-na-bar)
  When I first arrived in Bali to launch *Essential Bali*, this was the second restaurant I reviewed. On the one hand it seems unfair that I was allowed to eat here without having to pay for the privilege. On the other that meal

remains the benchmark by which all others are marked and, if I am brutally honest, despite salivating my way through writing this section, it's this meal that burns brightest in the darkness of my memory. The setting is ridiculous; the Moroccan décor subtly stylish and the food that emanates from the open kitchen is of a ridiculously high standard.

Mozaic—Western / Asian fusion

(www.mozaic-bali.com/mozaic-restaurant)
One of the jewels in Bali's heavily studded gastronomic crown, Mozaic has a reputation that stretches far beyond the shores of the small island it calls home. The setting is simply exquisite, a garden that feels sophisticated, classy and intimate. The food exceeds it; a constantly changing tasting menu that evolves according to the availability of ingredients and the moods of the chefs. Incorporating globally sourced quality with local produce, a meal here is both an experience and treat your tastebuds will remember for a long time.

That's not entertainment

t may be that I've just not been invited but entertaining at home is not a huge thing in Bali amongst the expat community. There are a couple of reasons why this is so. We've already mentioned the standard of kitchens in most villas is not quite up to what you'd expect to have elsewhere. Add in the fact that it can difficult to find high quality produce and the fact that it's almost as cheap to eat out as it is to eat in and generally eating out becomes the predominant way of socialising as opposed to hosting lavish dinner parties. Or, as I said, maybe I just don't have enough friends. Or maybe it's because I'm single and all the couples do the socialising.

LAZY SUNDAYS

Where there are expats, it seems, there are Sunday brunches. This isn't brunch as I used to define it—a combination of breakfast and lunch that generally came about as a result of not being bothered to get out of bed for the former and too hungry to wait for the latter. These are more of an event and a long-running one at that. They tend to start at 11 am or midday and stretch for three or four hours of all-you-can-eat and drink indulgence; a gluttonous way to spend your afternoon. Here are just a few options from the many on offer in Bali:

- **Feast**
  (www.sheratonbalikuta.com)
  The food at the Sunday Market Brunch is good without being anything completely spectacular. The fact you can take away a bag full of fresh market produce is a nice add-on, the live music is enjoyable but in all honesty it's the fact they have a freeflow champagne package at great rates that make it here. Sign up online for Starwood Preferred Guest membership and you get 30% off your bill.

- **Soleil**
  (www.themulia.com/en/soleil)
  If you want gluttony, then here you get gluttony. Soleil sits near the beachfront at the Mulia, consistently ranked one of the world's best beach resorts. It's grandiose and so is the brunch—I actually felt like they were fattening me up for the slaughter at one point. It's far from the cheapest option, but then you probably won't need to eat for a week afterwards.

- **Prego**
  (www.westinnusaduabali.com/en/prego-brunch)
  The Westin's addition to the brunch scene is remarkable

mainly for its laidback atmosphere that comes as a result of being specifically tailored towards families, with loads of kids' activities and entertainment to keep the little ones happy while you're filling your face. There's a lot of variety to the food so if you have little ones in tow then it's the place to aim for.

- **Kayu Putih**

  (www.kayuputirestaurant.com)

  I'll be honest this isn't my favourite; this is my aspiration. Because whenever I ask Bali veterans which is the best brunch on the island they always plump for the Astor Diamond Champagne Sunday Brunch and the name kinda gives away the reason why. This isn't an everyday brunch, this is a splash out; sign the bill without looking at what you've just spent and just enjoy the decadent brunch.

- **Nikki Beach Bali**

  (www.nikkibeach.com/destinations/beach-clubs/bali/)

  This is one for the beautiful people. Nikki Beach is synonymous around the world with beachside decadence and style and its arrival in Bali in 2015 caused quite the buzz. I can't quite vouch for its claim to be "the best brunch in the world" as we'd need to do considerably more research but as a stylish venue to enjoy and relax in post indulgence, I can't think of many better.

KEEPING IT REAL

We've covered the street food and we've explored the opposite end of the food spectrum, but there's perhaps one other experience that deserves to be on the top table. And it is an experience as much as a meal; indeed you could argue that for defining Bali it is as quintessential as they come. Jimbaran Bay is situated south of the airport, an extended crescent shape stretch of beach that has a couple of high-end resorts at one end, some basic *warungs* dotted around and towards the north end, a variety of seafood restaurants. Jimbaran is where the majority of the island's fishermen sell their booty and while the very best stuff is snapped up by the island's five-star establishments, there's more than enough to go round. The seafood restaurants here have their tables on the beach and are ideally positioned to make the very most of the island's sunsets. So picture this: you're seated at a candlelit table with your toes in the sand, an ice-cold Bintang in your hand. The sun is doing its magic in front of you and a plate full of the ocean's bounty appears on your plate just yards from the place it was landed that morning. The restaurants themselves are not high-end, the food is good without being great and the experience is one not to miss out on.

Taxes and tipping

Bali is one of those annoying places where you generally have to do some of your own maths to work out the cost of something. That's because the price you are quoted on a food menu will be augmented with Government Tax and service charges that will typically add up to anywhere between 15 and 21 per cent.

One question that bugged me for a long time was whether the service charges actually end up in the pockets of those who deserve it or, as has been reported for various Western establishments, a lot of it just goes towards the owners. It was a nice surprise to find that it's strictly adhered to that staff share the service money. Apparently that can also create issues when a 'casual' worker is offered a full-time job as the pot has to be split further, but you can be safe in the knowledge that money is going to the right person.

Not that this means you can't add on your own tip. Workers in Bali are typically paid very little so adding a few thousand Rupiah here and there will always be welcomed.

Joar Nicklas Brundin came to Bali in 2015. Here, he tells us why:

Food. One of the main reasons we chose to move to Bali was the food. It is an island where people from all over the world come to holiday and to eat well.

Bali itself starts with a really nice cuisine and very fresh produce. The volcanic soil is extremely fertile and grows a wide range of fruit and vegetables—including chilli. In Bali you also have a large influx of people from other Indonesian islands bringing their food with them—Javanese, Sumatran, Papuan and so on. Add this to the local dishes like suckling pig (*babi guling*) or amazing duck and you have a great diverse food culture before even looking at the Western restaurants.

Add some great international chefs coming to Bali to cater for the several million tourists each year and life is great. It is not surprising the best restaurants in Indonesia are in Bali.

Since produce and trained kitchen staff are inexpensive we get top class European food such as French cuisine, including foie gras or snails, for a fraction of what you would pay in France. Having previously lived in Sydney and Stockholm where the food is good but very expensive, it is great to be able to run out for a three-course lunch at a top restaurant with, say, a tuna tartar, grilled snapper and chocolate mousse for US$ 11.

Hungry and like local food? US$ 1 gets you some very nice chicken satay. US$ 4 a suckling pig banquet.

If we only had a few good vineyards in Bali it would be perfect. Yes, good wine is very expensive.

Living in a coffee producing country means we have lots of options and different types of freshly locally roasted coffees. I have learned which blends work best in a latte, which in an espresso, or in an affogato (they are very different). With a large Italian, French and Australian expat community the standard of baristas is also high.

The drawback to living with the abundance of good food is that it is hard to be motivated to eat and cook at home. When we first arrived we were eating out at least two of three meals. Some of our friends living here long-term do not even have stoves as they always eat out.

Eventually even I got tired of gravlax eggs benedict, blueberry pancakes or chorizo chatchuka for breakfast every day, and in the warmth it is hard to burn the same amount of calories as during a Swedish winter.

My wife is also a very good cook, so we have now pulled back and only eat out once a day. The sacrifices we make. Of course, this is in addition to going out for coffee or gelato.

Yes, the food is one very large reason we live in Bali.

Adam Baxter is an Australian who managed Bali classics Mama san and Sarong before branching out on his own to open GRAIN in central Seminyak. This is his story:

Running a restaurant is a dynamic, fun and fast changing environment. It is one of the few industries in the world where customers will tell you immediately if they like or dislike your product. The advantage of this, if you are prepared to adapt and change, is that you can improve your offerings quickly and see immediate growth.

In Bali we have an ever-changing customer base. The game here is to get into people's heads before they leave their home city to travel to Bali. Most people come with a 'must-do list' and to be successful you need to get your business on that list.

The reason this list exists in the first place is due to the abundance of wonderful restaurants here in Bali. There are a lot of options and that makes it tough for anyone to stand out and compete. In order to stay ahead you need to develop a whole plan of attack, from great food and coffee (in GRAIN's case), to a strong social media presence and marketing initiatives, to good old hustling to get customers from people walking by. It is not simply a matter of kicking the doors open and watching people flood in anymore; maybe it was like that five or more years ago, but these days you need to be improving all the time and coming up with different ways to get the word out there.

Getting people through the door is often the hardest part, because they have so many places to choose from. The word of mouth and goodwill necessary for a busy restaurant takes time to build and needs to be at the forefront of your motivations on a daily basis. You constantly have to reinvent your business; if you can manage to do all of this, and have a bit of fun along the way, then it really is a rewarding experience, as you get to see your business grow over time.

I'm often asked if it is difficult to start a business in Bali, and my standard answer is that I believe it is difficult to start a business anywhere. There are challenges unique to Bali, but on the other hand some things are easier.

In Bali, we are blessed with the ability and means to be as creative as we wish with our businesses. There are not really many limits upon what can be done. Also there is an abundance of fresh local and organically grown produce that we have access to.

It also brings you into contact with just about everybody, from other business owners, designers, musicians and artists to the more corporate crowd. In Bali, we meet a lot of tourists, who themselves come from a hugely diverse background.

Food has always been a great connector… after all, everyone has to eat.

CHAPTER 7

EXPLORING PARADISE

> ❝Sitting on a beach in Bali
> Tried to reach and grab a cloud
> Looked so much like cotton candy❞

—Joe Jackson, It's a Big World

TREASURE ISLAND

Speak to any Bali veteran and they all seem to have the same piece of advice for people who are new to the island. Get out of the place you are staying in, leave the metropoles (I use the term loosely) and explore the rest of the island. I hate the use of the term 'real Bali' because real is what you make it, but it's true to say that while the tourist centres offer a great deal in terms of eating out, shopping and beach life, to fully appreciate Bali you need to get out and explore it.

I'll start with a whistle stop tour round the island and then we can return for more leisurely visits to some of the main attractions. I've touched elsewhere on the tourist epicentre that is a strip of the south-western coast incorporating Kuta, Legian, Seminyak and Canggu, while elsewhere Nusa Dua in the south is home to the majority of super resorts. Each has their charm, but each is exactly the place those Bali veterans encourage you to leave.

One place that tops most people's list for a visit is the island's spiritual centre of Ubud. It, too, is a popular place to reside and offers a different vibe to the coastal hot spots. It's only 30 km (18.6 miles) north of Seminyak but feels like a world apart. Renowned as a hub where yoga and healthy living are the orders of the day, it 'benefited' from a worldwide publicity campaign in the form of the 2010 movie, *Eat, Pray, Love,* and the popularity of the book of the same name.

I placed the word 'benefited' with single quotes there on purpose because I am not sure that is entirely the case. The area of Ubud is undoubtedly still spectacular with rolling vistas of rural Bali. But the town itself, in my humble opinion, now suffers from its popularity. The roads to get there are always busy and the town always seems to be jammed full of tourists. I was in Ubud on my brief visit to the island in 2010 and it was what it said on the tin, a chilled, laidback town at peace with itself. Now, I am not convinced.

Further north is the volcanic theme park that is Mounts Kintamani and Batur, craters within craters, each with a destructive history, with lakes and various levels of flora. The outer craters are liberally dotted with restaurants with views across the calderas. The more adventurous might choose a day canyoning in this area. I did once and had the time of my life, culminating in a truly unique (and the latter word is one I never use loosely) experience. After a day of jumping into pools, abseiling and sliding my way down a canyon it came to our final obstacle, the GitGit waterfalls. This beautiful 35-m (114.8-ft) dual waterfall is an attraction in its own right, but it's much more fun to see it when you've just felt its raw power while trying to negotiate your way down it. And if you happen to do that negotiating while the Balinese are having a ceremony in the cave below, dressed in their finery and paying their respects to the gods while you're dressing in a wetsuit paying your respect to the waterfall, it's a moment you'll take to the grave; an archetypal 'only in Bali' moment.

Our journey around Bali thus far is neatly dividing the island in two so we may as well finish the dissection by ending up in Lovina, a sleepy seaside area on the northern coast most renowned for early morning trips to hang out with the dolphins. If we turn east at this point and start working our way along the coastline we will begin to encircle Mount Agung, situated on the eastern side of the island overlooking all that goes on beneath. There are several places of interest on the east coast, one of which is Tulamben. A truly unremarkable village hides its attraction under the waves. The USAT Liberty was originally beached here after being attacked and damaged during World War II, allowing its precious cargo to be rescued. And there it sat until Agung erupted in 1963 and the movement of the earth caused the ship to slide into the sea. The subsequent artificial reef is one of the world's most accessible shipwrecks for both divers and snorkelers.

The coastal towns of Amed and Candidasa are laidback, quiet places where it's easy to forget you're on the same island as Kuta and Seminyak, while for more peace and quiet an inland diversion to Sidemen offers peaceful tranquillity among the rice fields that lie in the shadow of Agung. Then there's Padangbai, a port that for a long time was the merely a jumping off point for trips to the outer islands that has now become a resort in its own right.

This bring us back to the centre of Bali civilisation with Sanur and beyond it the Bukit peninsula. And with that we've quickly done a semi-circle of the island. West of our imaginary line through the middle of the country is largely an unspoilt wilderness, ideal for trekking, exploring the West Bali National Park or snorkelling off deserted beaches. Many of the island's most sacred sites lie here, including Tanah Lot, the famous island temple that is a poster 'boy' for the island.

So much for the whistle stop tour, but let's take the time to spend a bit longer in a few places. I'm not going to beat about the bush here. I don't know a single expat who spends any time at all in Kuta. (Actually a caveat is one of my football mates who loves going out there but while I love him dearly he's something of a wrong 'un.) I don't want to upset people who love the place but while it does have its attractions those who live here tend to leave the place to the holidaymakers. OK, we're snobs—I can live with that. That isn't to say it doesn't have its highlights: Jamie Oliver opened a restaurant here (much to the bemusement of many expats) and the main Kuta seafront boasts some high-end hotels and restaurants. And if late nights partying are your thing then is the place to be, with notorious nightclubs such as Skygarden and Engine Room.

Seminyak is Kuta's more upmarket cousin. It's here you'll find the culinary epicentre of the island with an insane amount of quality eating establishments. Its upmarket credentials continue to grow; Ku De Ta beach club is an institution but is now challenged as a trendy spot with Potatohead and the W Hotel. You can also keep it real—beanbags on the beach with a cold bottle of Bintang never gets old. The streets are always busy but that's not to say you can't find peace and quiet here; with villas tucked away down every gang you can find your solitude with the bars and restaurants on your doorstep. It's also a big shopping environment.

Sandwiched between Kuta and Seminyak is Legian and the easiest way to describe it is to say that is not only halfway between its neighbours geographically but also in terms of style. Some trendy shops, some tat shops, some cool places to eat, some dodgy places. And to be completely frank the lines between all three of these neighbourhoods are becoming blurred. They are tourist centres and while I choose to live in Seminyak I do so down a quiet gang so I have it on my doorstep if I need but if I don't want to do battle with the tourist hordes I don't have to.

The majority of my friends still think this marks me out as strange because pretty much every one of them lives in Canggu and if the towns I have mentioned already are tourist hubs then this is truly an expat hub. People started to move here as a nice quiet alternative to Seminyak when the latter became more crowded, but while it retains its relatively quiet charm it's also something of a victim of its own success. More restaurants, bars and businesses open up every day and it is very communal but it's also getting busier and busier.

That's something nobody could really accuse Sanur of. On the east coast of the island, this is a sleepy town, lacking in the obvious culinary and more raucous delights of its eastern neighbours. If you want to chill out then this is a good place to do it in a village environment.

As I've already outlined, Ubud used to boast that as well, but while it is now a lot busier it does have it attractions. The Royal Palace is one, while Monkey Forest is another that draws the crowds. Watching the monkeys is amusing, watching naïve tourists ignore the warnings to look after their belongings is perhaps even more so. Another popular activity is white water rafting on the Ayung River — a great day out but choose your company carefully as some are more reputable than others. It's on a rafting trip where you'll really start to appreciate the main reason to go to Ubud, which is to explore the surrounding area. You don't need to go far out of the town itself to find yourself in a Balinese paradise and that's when you can truly appreciate it. A cycle trip or hike is a great way to enjoy nature as it was intended.

On the peninsula at the southernmost tip of the island you'll generally find the huge resorts. Nusa Dua is a completely artificial construct created for the tourist industry. It has nice, clean beaches with tranquil water and while the resorts have not outgrown the gated entity of Nusa Dua it's a place where people go to enclose themselves in a resort environment.

RIDING THE WAVES

If you live in Bali, or stay in Bali, and appreciate the high-class hotels, restaurants and various activities and attractions, then you've got surfing to thank. Whether you choose to try your luck on a board or not, the reality is that Bali's reputation as a surfing mecca is one that started the whole tourism boom.

The story of surfing on Bali goes back to 1936 when a young American photographer and surfer, Bob Koke, arrived in Bali with his longboard. He is renowned as the first surfer on Bali, the first of millions. He and his wife left the island in 1942 to escape the imminent arrival of the Japanese and it wasn't really until a few decades later that the rest of the world worked out what he had—that the surfing here is excellent.

The 1960s saw a steady trickle of surfers arriving to explore the island and this trickle grew to a steady stream in the 1970s. Kuta beach, with its ideal beginner waves and beach breaks, became the epicentre of Bali tourism, littered with cheap hotels and *warungs*—no five-star hotels or world-class restaurants for these early pioneers. It was a place for people to come on the cheap and indulge their passion for catching waves.

The popularity of surfing led to the tourism explosion here, but also led to the creation of a cottage industry, of board makers, board fixers, surf wear and surf schools. It's a great place to try surfing if you've never dabbled before so while I haven't got hooked on it I did feel the urge to at least have a go while living here.

The first activity was done on dry land as I was introduced to the theory of surfing, but as with so many activities of this ilk, what you do in theory is about as relevant to what you have to do in situ as firing a gun on a range before going out to war. Standing up on dry land is quite easy, I've been doing it most of my life. But doing it while wave after wave is testing my balance in the middle of the ocean moved the goalposts somewhat.

After many attempts, some more successful than others, and swallowing the better part of the Indian Ocean, my first lesson ended with little evidence that I was made for this lark. Then it was back in the water for my second lesson with a little more success. Indeed, the successful runs began to outnumber the unsuccessful ones. At one point I got up three times on the bounce only to have to abort as my board carved an inexorable course towards someone else's (not always my fault I should add). I was still having my fair share of complete failures as well, but progress was being made.

And then time was called on my second hour and we wound down with some theory lessons, this time on wind, tide, rips and more. Time for a shower and to peruse the photos that had been taken— some of which made me look vaguely competent.

I had the afternoon and night off but when I awoke the following morning my ageing bones knew they'd been busy doing something they weren't used to the previous day. Nevertheless, I was anxious to find out what a new dawn and new lesson would bring and it's fair to say the learning curve was about to steepen dramatically.

Reporting back to Ripcurl HQ I met Tito, my instructor for my third and final lesson. His was a no-nonsense approach. After a quick warm up he appraised the boards and the beach, shrugged his shoulders and said, "Let's just get out there and do this." 'This' was not the close inshore white water surfing of my initial attempts, but more like the real deal. We were paddling out to sea "to pick up a big wave". I didn't in all honesty think my efforts of the previous day had remotely qualified me for that, but in for a penny, in for 20,000 Rupiah.

Now I am here to tell you this. If you've ever looked at surfers and thought that the glory part looks amazing but all that hard work to paddle out to the waves looks like, well, hard work, you're dead right. To get over the incoming waves you have to lift the nose. If it breaks just in front of you, then you have to do an eskimo roll so the wave breaks over you as you're underneath your capsized board.

All this I gathered as I tried to paddle my way beyond where the waves were breaking. Writing it is a hell of a lot easier than doing it.

Eventually we made it out to a less tumultuous part of the ocean and sat on our boards. Of everything we did I found this annoyingly hard as I always seemed to be on the edge of losing my balance. A further part of my crash course involved turning the board to face the shore rather than the oncoming waves. It took some time and various calamities before we got to the stage where I was ready to actually catch a wave.

And there was, of course, the sinking feeling that considering I was still an absolute amateur, all of that hard work would be wasted as soon as I tried to stand up—an art I had far from mastered yesterday. Still, Tito spotted a wave and told me to start paddling, slowly at first and then harder. And then a miracle happened. As the wave caught my board I heard the cry to stand up and I jumped to my feet, established my balance and rode that beautiful wave all the way into the shore. I really did. I don't how or why I managed to do it, but I did. And it was beautiful. I was surfing and for the interminably few seconds I stood on that board being propelled to shore by the power of the waves, I got it. OK it wasn't exactly Bells Beach and I hadn't suddenly been transformed into a real surfer. But it was my wave, I caught it and it felt amazing.

There's a wonderful quote on surfing from an Australian singer-songwriter Xavier Rudd who says, "To surf, you're riding a pulse of energy from Mother Nature… You might be the only person in the history of the universe that connects with that particular pulse of energy." Riding that single wave as though I vaguely knew what I was doing, that resonated.

In truth that was as good as it got for the day. The rest of the lesson consisted of fighting against the waves that had for a fleeting moment given me so much pleasure. But I had my moment banked safely. And whether I ever catch another wave again, and I really hope I do, I will always have that one, the one that no one else will ever have and that, surely, is what surfing is all about.

NAMASTE

Bali is as synonymous with yoga as it is with surfing. It has become a favoured destination for yoga lovers, whether they indulge in regular classes on holiday or take an extra step and visit for a yoga retreat. And if Bali is a favoured destination, then Ubud is the Mecca.

Ubud was where I had my brush with yoga at the Radiantly Alive studios. I went for a private class which kept me away from having to do it in a group of experts but it also meant I couldn't do much hiding away.

I had no idea what to expect. I knew at a very basic level what a yoga class would entail, but what would I get the chance to do in one hour? Quite a lot, as it happened. We eased into a serious of poses and breathing exercises, many of which were familiar in name and ones that many people would recognise. I will never forget the time a man said, "you have a great downward dog" to me for the first time. Before long I was sweating but enjoying pushing my body into places it just wasn't used to going in. My instructor Rusty was enthusiastic, insisting that I had a great core and was made for yoga, although I insisted that he probably says that to all the boys. We smashed through some fundamental poses—the downward dog, the warrior, the child's pose and the crow. It sounds like the line-up from a children's adventure film but it's actually the building blocks of yoga.

Having done some basics we also dipped our toes in a few different styles; Osina, Restorative, Supta, Buddha Konasan and finally Roll and Release Yoga which is Rusty's personally tailored speciality. It entails the use of two tennis balls that are placed behind the shoulders or under your backside and a sequence of moves creates an intense massage effect. Apart from the end of the class that is spent in a recovery position relaxing and breathing to allow your body to recover it was a pretty full on hour and I could feel my body stretching out in a great way. I'd really enjoyed the session and enjoyed a second with a different teacher. It's far from straightforward and there are so many styles that to truly find 'my' yoga I would have to try other classes. As with surfing it's not a hobby I took any further than initial lessons, but it was still an enjoyable experience and if you're not going to try it here then you're really unlikely to try it anywhere.

GOING UNDER

I've already waxed lyrical about one diving experience of Tulamben, but there's far too much on offer to limit your diving experiences to the USAT Liberty and if you've never dived before then this is a perfect place to learn.

There's a financial benefit in that learning here is cheaper than many other parts of the world; there's an aesthetic benefit as it's so beautiful underneath the waves; there's a

variety benefit as there are so many places around Bali to dive, each with its own magical allure. And there's the fact that you're on Bali so when you're not diving you get to do everything else I've written about in this book.

The Gili Islands is a favourite place to learn with a litany of schools on the main drag; Nusa Penida and Nusa Lembongan also have schools but Bali itself also has a proliferation. Putting your head under water and trying to tell yourself to breathe (you can forget most of the theory but that's the one bit you can't manage without) blows your brain somewhat and it will take you a while to work out your buoyancy and how not to go through all the air in your tank faster than an asthmatic ant with some heavy shopping (couldn't resist that Blackadder line) but the staggering beauty of what you will see as a result is worth the financial and mental investment.

ADRENALINE RUSH

Still not enough for you? Well if you're still looking for a reason to get off your backside and do something exciting there are plenty more options on offer. Water has been something of a theme already, what with the surfing and the diving, but it's not just on the sea you can be at one with good old H_2O. There's plenty of fun to be had messing about on the river as well.

The mighty Ayung river winds its way through central Bali, carving an ever deepening niche in the valley. Ayung means beautiful and the river lives up to its name. And the best way to appreciate that beauty is from ground, or water level, with some white water rafting. The river is relatively gentle so this is suitable even for those faint of heart and it's a hell of a lot of fun. Watch out for the safety aspect though. Bali Adventure Tours (www.baliadventuretours.com) is one of the more reputable companies that do this trip and the great thing about using them is that you can also combine the rafting with another activity, such as mountain biking, a trip to the Elephant Sanctuary or trekking.

Another great day out for those with an adventurous mind, and another that allows you to truly appreciate Bali off the beaten track and end up splashing around, is quad biking and tubing. Spend the morning exploring the countryside on quad bikes and buggies, before an afternoon spent on a tiny dinghy ambling down a small river getting right back to nature. There are enough rapids to get your heart beating, enough slow parts to relax and go all floaty. I love this stuff anyway but what made it more special was spending time with the local guides who clearly love their jobs—and why wouldn't they? See baliquad.com for more.

If water isn't your thing, what about getting your feet away from both the wet stuff and terra firma? If you fancy making

Splashing out: Whether you're rafting or tubing, a day on the river is always great fun.

like Tarzan for the day head up to the Botanical Gardens in Bedugul and you'll not only get a chance to explore the gardens themselves but enjoy an adrenaline-charged thrill at the Bali Treetop complex (www.balitreetop.com). Replete with flying foxes, scramble nets and a variety of other obstacles positioned several feet above the safety of earth it's not for the fainthearted, but with a variety of courses graded according to difficulty, it's great fun.

...AND RELAX

If everything I have described so far seems far too much like hard work then worry not, for Bali is generally a peaceful place and while I love doing fun activities I'm also quite happy lying down doing absolutely nothing while getting a massage. And why wouldn't I be—there are so many options.

Spas in Bali run the entire range, beginning with cheap places where you can spend an hour getting treated for a few dollars, to exceptional luxury spas where you can pay hundreds for a day of complete pampering. You really do get what you pay for — the cheap establishments that you'll see everywhere eschew the luxuries and fripperies so you won't have your own room, the massage will be done fully clothed and the quality of massage might not be the best. Which is not to say it will be rubbish so don't dismiss them out of hand.

It's worth pointing out that while Bali isn't quite the world of happy endings that you associate with places like Thailand, that doesn't mean the concept is completely alien, especially in some of the more downmarket establishments. Avoiding that awkward moment is a matter of judgement and choosing a place that doesn't go in for that type of thing. I had one female friend who had a man come to her hotel room to give her a massage and she was rather surprised when he, shall we say, offered more than she had bargained for at the end of it. But generally the majority are there to give a cheap, decent service and there's nothing wrong with that.

At the other end of the spectrum there are the luxury spas. These are a different beast entirely, where serenity rules and from the moment you walk in the door you're wrapped in a cocoon of peace and pampering. They boast private rooms with great facilities where you'll be asked to change into paper pants and robes before foot washing ceremonies preceding the treatments. No matter how much you pay for your treatment the paper pants are probably the least flattering and comfortable things you'll ever have to wear, but they do the trick.

The really high level places will also have hydrotherapy facilities with spas, saunas and pools to really add the icing on top. There is a middle ground and if you stay here a long time it's one you'll probably explore. Jari Menari means dancing fingers and offers one of the best massages on the island without all the bells and whistles but with everything you need, while there are a variety of places that will dole out an hour of power for around US$ 20 that while not in the Rolls-Royce bracket, will offer a level of service that would cost considerably more back home. As I am fond of pointing out, when your eyes are closed it's what's going on with the treatment that is all-important. The writing of this book was aided by frequent relaxation sessions. In fact, I'm going for one now…

IN THE SWING

People relax in different ways and I know many men who have never been for a massage in Bali. But they do find walking around for a few hours hitting a ball with a stick to be a way of letting it all out. Each to their own.

While Bali is renowned for its surf, culture, history, yoga, temples and spas, it's not famous for golf, although it does have some wonderful courses. The three main courses are Nirwana Bali Golf Club, situated some 25 km (15.5 miles) north of the airport close to the famous Tanah Lot temple; Bali National Golf in Nusa Dua; and New Kuta Golf Club, around 15 km (9.3 miles) south of the airport on the way to Ulawatu. Together they form a high-quality trio of courses with differing challenges, stunning views and wonderful welcomes.

Bali's best-known course is a 20-year-old sensation designed by Greg Norman and it boasts one of the most photographed golf holes in the world. Any golf course that benefits from rugged coastline automatically inspires awe and wonder, but when you've also got Tanah Lot temple as a part of the backdrop it's something completely unique in the world of golf. There are three clifftop holes played parallel to the waves of the Indian Ocean crashing on the shore in as dramatic a setting as any you will find.

Highlights of the course include rice terraces on the first hole and a tee shot across the surf on the seventh. It is this hole that showcases Tanah Lot making it one of the most memorable holes any golfer will have the privilege to play.

Around 35 km (21.7 miles) to the south, New Kuta is Bali's newest course, under a decade old. Located at Pecatu on the Bukit Peninsula, the area surrounding the course is undergoing huge development with numerous new hotel and accommodation developments underway that will put this course right in the middle of a new boom area.

Not that it is lacking anything at the moment in pure golfing terms, offering a challenging course and benefiting, like Nirwana, from its coastal location. The front nine is in a natural tropical lowland setting with creeks, long grasses, scrub and creepers. It's a great course until this point, but on the back nine it really comes into its own as every swing of your club brings you closer to the clifftop coastline. The 14th takes you up to it while the signature 15th hole, named the Cliffhanger, allows you to fully appreciate the majesty of the Bali coastline while you'll happily allow your playing partners all the time in the world to play their tee shots at 16 in order for you to enjoy the magnificent view.

Bali National Golf Club (formerly known as the Bali Golf & Country Club) is nestled into a corner of the Nusa Dua complex that is home to a wide array of five-star hotels boasting some of Bali's finest accommodation. Eighteen months of work went into a recent reimagining of the course and the results are fantastic. Much of the course was merely remodelled keeping faithful to the original design, but some new elements have improved the course immeasurably. BNGC does not benefit from hugging the coastline, but on a clear day you'll revel in a view of Mount Agung in the distance and the course itself is simply immaculate.

A WALK IN THE PARK

I've had cause to mention Mount Agung and its smaller brethren several times throughout this book. And I haven't even got to the best bit about the volcanoes—climbing them. Anyone can watch a sunset in Bali, on your backside sipping a cocktail and watching the end of another glorious day. But to enjoy the sunrise you need to get up early, and to really enjoy it you need to get up earlier than that and put some hard yards in to appreciate it from the top of a mountain.

Climbing Agung is not for the fainthearted or weak of spirit. It's a good five- to six-hour climb so my earlier comment about getting

Lazy guides will take you straight down from the top but make sure if you're up to it that you walk around the rim of the crater—the views are simply brilliant and if you've made it that far then you may as well make the most of it.

up early is actually largely irrelevant as you probably won't get to bed at all. It's tough, but if you want to take the plaudits for beating Bali when it comes to adventure then it's the climb for you. For an easier climb (and a more realistic one for most) try Mount Batur. Everything is relative—I found it fairly easy but I've spoken to many who still class it as tough. But eminently doable no matter what physical state you're in. And the views from the top are worth any discomfort.

HOLY GROUND

As we've already ascertained, there are rather a lot of temples in Bali. But while the vast majority are much of a muchness there are a handful that are anything but and well worth a specific visit to enjoy.

Tanah Lot (ancient land) is perhaps the most famous,

and almost certainly the most photographed, temple in Bali. Fifteen km (9.3 miles) north of Seminyak, it emerges from the seabed and can only be accessed on foot at low tide, although you can't enter unless you're Balinese so while some still like the opportunity to get up close and personal, I'd recommend a visit when the tide is high so that you can appreciate the temple in its imposing island glory. The other benefit is that your view of the temple isn't obscured by hundreds of fellow tourists.

Without being able to access the temple itself the real experience here is to walk along the clifftops liberally dotted with other, smaller temples and the main event every day is sunset. Bali is hardly lacking in wonderful locations to watch the source of our heat slip beneath the horizon at the end of the day, but this, understandably, is an eternal favourite. Getting to Tanah Lot a couple of hours before sunset, doing your exploring and then bagging yourself a prime spot at one of the many cafes and bars on the clifftop to the south is not the worst idea.

Tanah Lot is one of seven sea temples founded in the 16th century by a Majahapit monk from Java by the name of Niratha. The temples form a chain around the island and from Tanah Lot a gaze south-east on a clear day would line up Pura Luhur Uluwatu, on the island's south-westernmost tip. *Ulu* means head, while *watu* means rock. Luhur apparently means heavenly, ancestral, original and transcendent. This sprawling edifice built on the headland is a remarkable construction and a visit offers a completely different experience than that offered by Tanah Lot.

Having paid your entrance fee you will be given either a sash or a sari dependent on your attire and this must be worn appropriately during your visit. While Tanah Lot is a small self-contained temple, Uluwatu is more of a complex that you are allowed to explore without barriers except for the small inner temple. Once you've become used to the monkeys that abound at this site and think nothing of approaching you and stealing anything they can get their claws on—including sunglasses—you'll have time to pay attention to the coral brick walls covered in elaborate carvings.

You can walk around the main building area but the real beauty here lies in the pathways that extend both left and right along cliffs. Below you'll find mesmerising views of the Indian Ocean crashing onto the rocks below. Looking back to the temple you'll marvel at stunning landscapes where the man-made seemingly merges into the natural splendour of

the undulating coastline. There's a small network of pathways and it's worth taking the time to explore them all as it's a good opportunity to escape the crowds and enjoy some peaceful time at this spiritual centre.

While it doesn't have the magic allure of Tanah Lot that sits between you and the setting sun, this is still a spectacular place to watch the orb go down and a visit at that time will also enable you to take in the popular Kecak dance held within the grounds at this time of day.

Five other temples worth visiting

1. Pura Besakih—also known as the Mother Temple. Located on the slopes of Mount Agung, it is the largest and most important temple of the Hindu religion in Bali. It is actually network of over 20 temples that date back to prehistoric times. When Mount Agung erupted in 1963 the lava flow just missed the temple.

2. Pura Goa Lawah—It's unlikely you'd make a trip specifically to see this temple but if you're journeying along the east coast it is worth a stop off. The temple itself is unremarkable but it is the setting and tenants that make it stand out. The temple is in a cave full of thousands of bats (and a few snakes) that lend an interesting aroma to proceedings.

3. Pura Taman Ayun—Thanks to its location 18 km (11.2 miles) north-west of Denpasar, Pura Taman Ayun is a popular stop off for many organised tours heading north of the major tourist centres. Its defining characteristic is the lake, or moat, around it that gives the impression of a temple floating on the water.

4. Gunung Kawi—The temple complex north-east of Ubud is famous for the ten shrines that are etched into the rock face. The ten shrines are each seven metres high and sit in depressions etched into the rock. A 300-step stone stairway is its other major feature.

5. Goa Gajah—Located close to Ubud, the 'elephant cave' has a wonderfully ornate façade depicting various creatures, none of which you'd consider taking home for a pet. The primary animal forming the entrance to the cave was thought to be an elephant, hence the name, but given the almost supernatural nature of the other carvings it's highly debatable.

DANCING SHOES

Balinese dance is a truly enchanting spectacle. In many ways it is the very epitome of Balinese culture and provides an opportunity for visitors to connect with tradition and history.

Everything about Balinese dance is elaborate, from the costumes to the exaggerated movements and heavy make-up, but it's the style of dancing that fascinates me. Every joint of the body seems to be utilised in each movement. Elbows protrude away from the body, wrists are bent back to an unnatural degree while the fingers are extended at seemingly impossible angles (take a look and try it yourself and you'll realise just how impossible).

Glance down and you'll notice similar dexterity in the feet, while the neck and waist movements are also exaggerated and extreme. To say every move is heavily choreographed is almost an understatement; each pose in the dance is created as several different body parts are reassigned into a new pre-set position with the result of a body shape metamorphosing before your eyes.

The protagonists are incredibly wide-eyed with pronounced, penetrating stares. On odd occasions a dancer's gaze will seem locked on yours and it is almost unnerving, daring you to look away before the moment is over and the dancer's scrutinising look will move elsewhere.

Their movements are carefully matched to the sounds of the gamelan, a traditional ensemble of percussion instruments that create an instantly identifiable style of music. The predominant instrument is the metallophone, a variation on the xylophone with tuned metal bars struck by mallets. 'Kendhang' drums are the other major contributor, while bamboo

The word 'gamelan' means 'to hammer' and it's easy to see why.

flutes and stringed instruments are sometimes utilised. Gamelan has its own place in the traditions and culture of Bali, but to see it combined with dance is to appreciate two major elements simultaneously. Now in the interests of brutal honesty I have to say I can't stand gamelan music. I can just about deal with it watching a dance but otherwise it leaves me cold, but that's a personal thing.

There's an incredibly diverse amount of Balinese dance, but the chances are if you do go to see one you'll end up watching one of the dance-drama classics of the island where the story behind the dance can be fascinating in itself.

Ramayana is one of the most prevalent tales accounting for more than one dance. With its roots as one of two Hindu epics, there are regional variations from the Indian original. Bali's sees the "good guys" Rama, Sita and Rama's brother

Laksamana in the jungle as the "bad guys" King Rahwana and his minister Marica of the Alengka kingdom plot to kidnap Sita. Luring Rama and then Laksmana away before tricking Sita, their plot is successful at first. Rahwana defeats giant bird Jayatu who attempts to foil the plot and gets Sita to his palace where he plans to force her into marrying him.

At this stage the hero white monkey, Hanoman, enters the fray. Tasked by Rama to meet Sita in exile he manages to make contact, eventually leading to a big showdown between the major protagonists whereby Rahwana is finally defeated and our heroes live happily ever after.

A fascinating variation on the Ramayana theme is the Kecak dance that is one of the most popular on the island. It tells much the same tale but its key feature is that it does not entail use of gamelan (which is a relief to me) but a choir that provides the entire soundtrack to the dance using a specific "cak" vocal sound. It's amazing to watch the dance, but even more fascinating to hear this strange vocal sound utilised to provide its entire soundtrack.

The Barong dance is another classic that draws on mythology and history to tell another stirring tale of good versus evil. There are many variations on the Barong dance but the basic story revolves around another pair of foes. In this the story goes that Rangda, the mother of Erlangga, King of Bali, is banished from the kingdom for practicing black magic. After becoming a widow she summons all the evils spirits from the jungle to fight Erlangga, who has to enlist the help of Barong in order to survive. Barong is a lion-esque creature usually played by two dancers at front and back of a wonderful 'costume'. He goes to fight Rangda with the help of Erlangga's soldiers but Ranga casts a spell over the soldiers that makes them suicidal and they attempt to kill themselves with their *kris* or dagger. Barong reacts with a spell of his own, making the soldiers invulnerable to sharp objects before going on to fight Rangda and defeat her.

Visitors to Ubud can visit the Royal Palace to see Balinese dance and it's an atmospheric place to indulge, if slightly touristy. You might want to seek out a smaller, more local performance. As I mentioned earlier you can also see the kecak at Uluwatu temple at sunset. Alternatively, many hotels offer the ability to enjoy Balinese dance while indulging in local food. Then there's the aforementioned Kecak dance that takes place at Pura Luhur Uluwatu (Uluwatu temple) daily at sundown; a breathtaking spectacle in a breathtaking venue.

MORE TO SEE

If you think I've covered off everything to do while you're in Bali you'd be wrong, very wrong. This isn't a place where you are going to run out of things to do in a hurry. Where there are tourists there are tourist attractions so while I've covered a lot of activities and cultural ideas, there are a lot of attractions to put on your lists as well.

Staying within the cultural remit for a while, however, there's a place called Taman Nusa in eastern Bali that is a fascinating live museum where the owners have literally collected old buildings from around Indonesia and created a village with them. It's an architectural and historical journey around the country and it's fascinating to see how the different islands evolved and the practical considerations that had to be taken into account when evolving building styles.

Sticking still further with the cultural theme the GWK Cultural Park is situated on the highest part of the southern end of the island with great views across it. The best view is that of Wisnu (Vishnu), a statue of the Hindu god that looks over the island. The original plan was that Wisnu would be atop his mythical creature Garuda (the name of Indonesia's national airline) but the grand plans for this and the rest of the park got shelved, leaving a feeling of a half-completed job. But the project was reinvigorated lately so the statue should be completed as first envisaged and added to with other exhibits and cultural shows. In truth the views alone are a good enough reason to visit. (It's also another venue that offers the opportunity to watch Balinese dance.)

If local wildlife is your thing then there's the Bali Safari and Marine Park and Bali Zoo, as well as the Elephant Safari Park. Personally I'm not a huge fan of zoos and the Bali Safari and Marine Park is not as far away from being a zoo as it likes to make out, but to be fair their breeding record is very good and recent additions have included a giraffe, a hippo and a white rhino. The Elephant Safari Park is a different and fascinating story. Some visitors and social media commentators bemoan the fact that the elephants are chained up at night, but the truth is they'd probably all be dead by now if they weren't here.

Owner Nigel Mason encountered a group of nine Sumatran elephants looking somewhat forlorn in a rice paddy and decided to create a sanctuary for them. Having decided to save nine, he then set his sights a bit higher.

The Sumatran elephant is a critically endangered species — one that has lost half of its population in one generation, predominantly due to a 70 per cent loss of habitat caused by the epic deforestation that goes on in Indonesia. On their home island many of the creatures are rounded up and left in 'Training Camps' where they are poorly looked after, so Nigel did what anyone would. He made room for them in his new park, went over to Sumatra, put them on the back of a lorry (several lorries) and drove them 3,000 km (1864.1 miles) to a new and better future in Bali. There was a two-year delay in the project and that delay only served to highlight the issues; half of the ten elephants originally selected were dead by the time it came to actually move them.

GOOD SPORT

We've touched elsewhere on the love of football on the island and it extends further than just playing on the beaches or futsal courts around the island. There's also passionate support of the local Bali FC team. Not that being able to support the team is a given as they actually have to be playing matches and that hasn't been straightforward. In 2015 the Indonesian FA was banned from international competition by FIFA for government interference. If you know anything about the beautiful game at all you will probably be picking your jaw up from the floor. To get banned, by FIFA, for interference. It sounds like a bad joke. An unofficial club competition did kick off in 2016 and literally the day before I wrote this sentence the ban was overturned. I have mates who are professional footballers here and it's not been a profitable time for them. But that should now be in the past and if you get chance to watch a game you'll be blown away by the passion shown by the fans here.

Away from football Bali is not a hugely sporty place; you won't see many sports facilities around. There's one cricket pitch but talking to my friends who play on it the bounce is, shall we say, variable. But everywhere has one sport that makes you go "huh" and in Bali that would probably be buffalo racing. This takes part mainly in the west of the island and sees people on small carts pulled by buffalo, erm, racing. Takes all sorts.

NO CARS PLEASE, WE'RE GILIS

The Gili Islands are actually a part of Lombok, but they have become synonymous with Bali and a classic getaway from daily Bali life. The three tiny islands boast a magnetism thanks partially to their Treasure Island mystique — all magical blue sea, golden sand and ripe for exploration. Above and beyond that is the fact that motorised transport is not allowed and only when you have inhabited such a place can you truly appreciate just how that can affect the pace of life and, subsequently, your mental state.

Everyone who comes here should avoid sticking just to one area. Don't just stay in Seminyak, Legian or Kuta and do your shopping and eating there. Explore different areas and go to the north where it is quieter and more genuine. My Bali secret, if people like outdoor activities, then I would recommend them to go the north of Bali and go trekking to some waterfalls that are not very well known in Sambangan. People are friendly and it is a bit challenging but there is natural beauty that has not been damaged yet and for people who love nature, that's what I would recommend.
– Thierry Gasnier, General Manager of the Kuta Beach Heritage Hotel

Strictly speaking the 'Gili Islands' is a misnomer as Gili simply means island in Sasak, the native language of Lombok. Gili Air is the closest to the 'mainland' and takes up the middle ground in terms of both size and liveliness. Meno is the next in line — the smallest island is also the quietest, a haven of total tranquillity and low habitation. Then there's Gili Trawangan (affectionately referred to as Gili T), just 3 km (1.9 miles) by 2 km (1.2 miles) but the largest of the trio. Renowned as a backpacker's paradise with a party scene to accompany the idyllic setting, there is much more to it and there's no reason tourists of any ilk cannot make the most of everything this tiny landmass has to offer.

The charm is immediately apparent upon arriving at Gili Trawangan after a 2½-hour speedboat ride from Benoa harbour. To get your feet wet is an idiom that means trying something for the first time and here it's a literal interpretation as disembarkation from the boat entails climbing down a ladder onto the beach as the waves gently lap against the shore, the water kissing your feet as they touch the island for the first time. You could probably get away with throwing your footwear away from this point onwards really; you'll barely require it.

A DROP IN THE OCEAN

As I highlighted in Chapter Two, Bali is just one small part of Indonesia and it's a great jumping off point to discover the rest of it. We've mentioned the magical Gili Islands but Lombok itself is also worth exploring whether to explore its own version of Kuta that is a lot less rowdy than the Bali version, climb Mount Rinjani or chill out in secluded surf towns.

Komodo is home to the famous dragons while islands like Flores attract people who want to enjoy a completely unspoilt landscape. West of Bali is Java and this huge island has its own attractions, from the volcanoes to cultural towns such as Yogyakarta and Surabaya.

LET'S CELEBRATE!

As we've already ascertained, the Balinese do love a ceremony. And that extends to various celebrations and festivals that take over the whole island and allow you to feel part of it.

Year-on-year—Galungan and Kuningan

These joint celebrations take place at the same time of every Balinese year—that is every 210 days. For Galungan you'll notice long bamboo sticks called *penjars*, lining the roads. They symbolise Mount Agung and are the thoroughfare for the gods to come and join the festivities. Ornaments are tied to them symbolising the crops. The gods hang around for ten days until Kuningan where temples are decorated with yellow fabric. The following day is a family day where the Balinese pay visits to the ones they love with gifts.

Enjoy the silence—Nyepi

If you're not already confused by Balinese ceremonies, Nyepi will probably finish you off. This one is celebrated according to the Hindu Saka calendar as opposed to the Balinese one and so occurs around March/April every year.

It begins with the procession of the Ogoh Ogoh, a procession of giant monsters made form bamboo and paper mache accompanied by a mighty racket with firecrackers, saucepans, cymbals and gongs making a noise to scare away the demons. With all the noise made, the following day of Nyepi itself is a day of silence and meditating. And they do mean silence; no travel is allowed and no electricity is to be used. And this applies to everyone. While there is an element of leeway within hotel complexes everyone in the island is banned from the roads (with the exception of emergency services) and local *banjars* enforce the rules if they see errant Westerners with lights on and televisions flickering.

Nyepi is the only event in the world that closes an airport for a day as no flights are allowed in or out of the island.

CHAPTER 8

HOW DO YOU SAY...?

> *Saya bisa bicara sedikit Bahasa Indonesia*
> *(I can speak a little bit of Indonesian)*

When it comes to speaking like the locals you first need to consider that not all locals speak the same language. There are three predominant languages in Bali: Balinese, Bahasa Indonesia and English. '*Bahasa*' is the Indonesian word for 'language' and while one of my expat friends gets ridiculously angry about the idea of referring to a language by the word 'language' it's what you'll hear most locals refer to it as, so that's what we'll do here.

If you choose to live in one of the main tourist areas, which most expats do, then the reality is that you can get away with barely knowing a word of the local languages. English will get you a long way, whether you're at a bar, in a taxi or saying hello to someone as you walk down the street.

But that's fundamentally boring and a tad disrespectful and as with every foreign territory the benefits of learning some basics of the language far outweigh the work involved. You do, though, have a choice of whether to concentrate on learning Balinese or Bahasa. Most people, myself included, choose Indonesian because it's the national language and is therefore much more practical. And as so many people on Bali are internal migrants, from islands such as Java, you might find Balinese actually restricts how many people you can converse with. After all, Balinese is one of over 700 languages spoken in Indonesia. I do have one Indonesian friend who once started speaking to a waitress in a bar who could not understand a word she said because the waitress in question was Balinese and had only ever bothered to learn English and not Indonesian, but that would be a rare thing indeed.

Bahasa Indonesia is a young language and came along as recently as 1945 on the back of independence as a way of bringing the country together under one linguistic roof. If you speak Malay then congratulations, you can probably skip this chapter as that's the source for most of Bahasa. Malay had already spread through the country during the reign of the Dutch so when looking for an official language it made sense to base it on that, despite the fact that at the time the country's most popular language was Javanese. It was also more politically expedient.

But because this is a language that was 'created' as opposed to evolved, there are differences and you'll also discover a few hangovers from the Dutch colonial rule in there, with some odd words that derive from other languages just to keep you on your toes. And if English is your first language then you'll be glad to hear there are a few words that will be very familiar (see page 173).

The good news is that Bahasa has a relatively simple structure; it's not quite a pidgin language, but there are no issues with feminine and masculine versions of words and, more importantly, no real tenses for verbs, so with a few exceptions once you have learned the verb you're pretty much set up to use it in any circumstances.

It's also an efficient language with lots of crossovers—the word *lagi* means 'again' or 'more', while *selamat* means 'safe' but can be used as the initial word in the sayings 'Happy birthday', 'Happy new year', 'Hello', 'Good morning', 'Good afternoon', 'Good evening' or 'Safe journey'. The way they create phrases can be quite amusing. 'To receive' plus 'love' (*terima kasih*) equals 'Thank you.' 'Heart' plus 'heart' (*hati-*

hati) equals 'Caution.' While 'ready' plus 'ready' (*siap-siap*) means 'getting ready.'

One thing that annoys me to this day is that for such a polite bunch of people they don't have a word for 'please'. So when asking for something it's not rude to just say what you want but it feels like that, especially when you're an overly polite Englishman. At the opposite end of the idiosyncratic scale there are very few negative words in Indonesian. There's no real word for 'bad'—instead you just say '*tidak bagus*'—not good.

Like all languages it has its illogical moments and times when it seems ridiculously inefficient, but overall you get a good bang for your learning buck.

WHERE CAN I LEARN?

You'll be able to pick up a few words quite easily but if you're serious about learning the language, and you really will reap the benefits, then you'll need to take lessons. There's only so far apps and online guides can take you but I think the most important part of lessons is that it enables you to talk to Indonesians, helping not only your understanding of the language but of the culture it represents. The lack of word for 'please' means I have always felt quite rude when asking for something in a bar, restaurant or shop, but I felt more comfortable having had the chance to discuss it with my teacher. There is a word for please—*Silakhan*—but this is used more at the beginning of a request such as "please close the door" rather than "could I have another Bintang please?" (The first thing I learned was "*satu lagi*" meaning "one more" which is a perfectly acceptable way of ordering that next Bintang.)

The Indonesian for 'hello' is 'halo'.

There are many language schools that will educate you but if you fancy something more concentrated in a more relaxed version it's also possible to have a personal tutor who will come to your home. That's the path I chose and found that it became a social experience as much as a learning one. With prices working out at around US$ 7.50 per hour a one-on-one set up in the comfort of your own home is an affordable and effective option.

A WORD TO THE WISE

Selamat	Safe
Pagi	Morning (sunrise — 11:00 am)
Siang	Daytime / Midday (11:00 am — 3:00 pm)
Sore	Afternoon (3:00 pm — sunset)
Selamat pagi	Good morning!
Selamat siang	Good day!
Selamat sore	Good afternoon!
Selamat malam	Good evening / night!
Halo	Hello
Apa	What
Kabar	News
Apa Kabar?	What's new / What's going on?
Terima	To receive
Kasih	Love (not romantic)
Terima Kasih	Thank you
Ya	Yes
Tidak	No
Saya	I, me, mine
Want	Mau
Ini	This
Itu	That
Perlu	Need
Mengerti	To understand
Bahasa	Language
Bahasa Indonesia	The Indonesian Language
Bahasa Inggris	The English Language
Anda / kamu	You
Bicara	To speak

Bisa	Can / To be able to
Dan	And
Saya dari Indonesia	I am from Indonesia.
Saya tidak mengerti Bahasa Indonesia	I don't understand Indonesian.
Anda bisa bicara Bahasa Inggris?	Can you speak English?

IT'S NOT JUST WHAT YOU SAY, IT'S HOW YOU SAY IT

Fortunately, there aren't too many idiosyncrasies when it comes to pronouncing Indonesian. It uses the Latin alphabet and overall can be depended on to have similar sounds to those you're used to. But there are a couple of curveballs to keep you on your feet.

Letter(s)	Sounds Like	Example(s)
A	AH	Rather
B	B	Bat
C	CH	China
D	D	Dog
E	E / EH [1]	Open or Elephant
F	F	Fruit
G	G	Get (never like J or dg)
H	H	Help (never silent, even if placed at the end of a word) [2]
I	EE / IH [3]	Greet, India
J	J	Jump
K	K /KH	Key, Loch
KS	X	Taxi
L	L	Lane
M	M	Middle

N	N	Name
NG	NG [4]	Sing
NGG	NG + G [5]	Finger (always pronounce second G)
O	OH	Tote
P	P	Packet
Q	K	Iraq
R	RR	Rolled 'r'
S	S	State
T	T	Toy
U	Oo	Boot
V	F, V	If or Vote
W	W	Where
X	X	Taxi (rare, KS more common)
Z	Z	Zebra

1. The letter E can be pronounced long or short but there is no written distinction. Most are pronounced short.
2. The letter H is always pronounced even if it is at the end of the word. A common example is when saying Thank you—'*Terima Kasih*'
3. The letter I can be long or short.
4. If only one G in an NG sound then it always soft, like 'singer' not 'anger'. For the harder sound of 'anger' this only occurs with two Gs—NGG.
5. Rolling your Rs is fun—if you can get the hang of it. There aren't any obvious examples in English using the letter R but it's similar to what you you do when pronouncing butter.

Double Vowels and the Glottal Stop

If there are two consecutive vowels in a word it requires a

glottal stop. Effectively there is an apostrophe between the two letters. For a good example think of how you would say Uh-oh or Oh-oh when warning of something amiss.

Words ending in K are usually pronounced with a glottal stop. The K at the end of a word becomes a hard stop at the back of the throat. An example of this is when you say No—*Tidak*.

NUMBERS GAME

When it comes to the numbers game there's nothing too complicated about Indonesia. Once you've got 1-9 in your brain and a couple of suffixes you're good to go. The nature of the Indonesian currency means that people generally drop three noughts off so 260,000 becomes 260.

Nomor	Number
Nol	Zero
Satu	One
Dua	Two
Tiga	Three
Empat	Four
Lima	Five
Enam	Six
Tujuh	Seven
Delapan	Eight
Sembilan	Nine
Belas	Suffix for –teen
(Se)puluh	10 / suffix for multiples of 10
(Se)ratus	100 / suffix for multiples of 100
(Se)ribu	1000 / suffix for multiples of 1000
Juta	Million

SPEAK LIKE A LOCAL

It is somewhat disingenuous of me to ignore the Balinese language completely and you've already picked up the odd word—bule is Balinese. Suksema is another good one to have up your sleeve—you can't learn to say thank you in too many languages.

The sad fact is Balinese is not exactly dying out but it's definitely in decline. This is largely a result of the urbanisation of the Balinese whereby Indonesian and English are the primary languages. Where Indonesian is relatively straightforward, Balinese has many quirks thanks to the variety of words needed based on the Balinese caste system that decrees you address people differently according to their status. Another difficulty for Westerners attempting to learn it is the hard pronunciation that comes partly as a result of the fact that the Balinese script does not translate to Latin very easily.

Sounds Familiar?

Here are some Indonesian words that derive from English:

- *alternatif*   alternative
- *aroma*   aroma
- *botol*   bottle
- *elektronik*   electronic
- *favorit*   favorite
- *informasi*   information
- *kamera*   camera
- *komputer*   computer
- *lokal*   local
- *musik*   music
- *panik*   panic
- *sama*   same
- *spesial*   special
- *telepon*   phone
- *tradisional*   traditional

CHAPTER 10

WORKING AND RUNNING A BUSINESS

> ❝He won't fly on the Balinese airline, Garuda,
> because he won't fly on any airline where
> the pilots believe in reincarnation.❞

– Spalding Gray

MAYBE ON TUESDAY

If you're going to work and manage a business in Bali there's one thing you're going to need in abundance: patience. It's probably a more valuable commodity than money in some ways. There are multitudinous examples of this that will inevitably come up in this chapter but to find out for yourself all you ever have to do is talk to someone who is trying to open a business in Bali. Whether it's a first-time business owner opening a small *warung* or the General Manager trying to open a new attraction the story is always the same. There's when you want to open, when you get told by your advisors you will open, when you readjust your ambitions to thinking you may open and, finally, many months after you thought you would, you finally open.

It became a standing joke at *Essential Bali* that whenever we talked to a business that was opening a new entity or someone opening a new place they'd tell us which month they were hoping to be in action and we'd query "which year?" The question was semi-sardonic and semi-serious. Every project goes over time here. And even when you're up and running, you'll need that patience when it comes to day-to-day workings.

All of which is a negative way to start a chapter so let's bring some joy and happiness, and dare we say it, enthusiasm into your life. For while patience is a commodity that merely takes inner control, money is a commodity to be earned or borrowed before you go into business and the good news is that your investment capital will go a lot further here than most places. My theory behind the explosion of the restaurant scene here goes thus: if you're a chef and you want to open your own place the cash you would need to open in Melbourne or Manchester would be hugely significant. Here you can do it all for a fraction of the cost and run it the same way. Material is cheap, labour is cheap, land is cheap. And you don't have to jump through the same level of Health and Safety regulations or various other hoops most Western civilisations now insist you jump through before opening any kind of business, especially in the service industry. And no one thinks the worse of you if you got into a business meeting wearing shorts and flip-flops either. You might stretch to a pair of linen trousers and a collar on your shirt, but if I have ever seen a man wearing a suit for business here I have forgotten it.

The first time I got chatting to the owner of my favourite restaurant here, Merah Putih, a friend asked if he had always dreamed of living in Bali and he replied negatively. Questioned further on what his dream was, he looked around his glorious establishment and said, "Open this place in London, but I'll never be able to afford that."

And that, in essence, is one of the main reasons this is a good place to start a business.

And it's really not all that difficult in terms of the initial bureaucracy. The hardest part, as we've already hinted, is finding a local that you trust enough to be the sponsor of your business. In theory they can just waltz in and take it all from you at the drop of a hat so finding someone you trust is key.

There is only one type of business that a foreigner can establish here and it's called a PT.PMA. The costs to set one up vary on the type of business you want to establish. (See 'Setting Up A Business' on page 182 for requirements.) It sounds relatively easy listed down and in truth it's not prohibitively difficult. The Indonesian government continually fluctuates between defending itself and its people from outside influence while encouraging foreign investment. So while there is a bit of red tape to go through it's realistically no more than any other country and if you have a good agency on your side to walk you through it, opening a business here is not so difficult. But having the right bits of paper is only the start of the battle.

We've touched on the vagaries of owning land and

buildings elsewhere in this book and it was confusing enough then without going into it all over again here but it's obviously going to be an issue if you want to open a restaurant or establishment here. For other businesses it's easy enough to rent office space or a building that can be used as an office.

Finding good staff to put in it can be more of a challenge. In truth there's a reality check to be had here. I look at how many top class hotels, restaurants and so on are now in Bali and always wonder how each finds enough good staff to provide the level of service required. This is no meant in any way to disparage the Balinese and Indonesians who staff them, but there's a huge cultural and experiential gulf between where they live and where they work. I discovered that one of the very expensive resorts I reviewed had an agreement with the local banjar that 80 per cent of its staff must come from that village. It's admirable but a huge challenge to the resort to create a level of service fit for rich foreigners from people whose life and worldly experience is very limited. Training is everything—some do it better than others.

There are other considerations you have to take into account when working out your staffing requirements—there's a stipulation that on their biggest religious holiday you pay them an extra month's wages for one. And as I've mentioned before, if one of your staff members has a village ceremony that will take precedence over coming in to earn a day's pay.

All of this comes under the umbrella of cultural appreciation that is required to do business or work here. You need to understand the nature and traditions of your staff but also the people you do business with. I never got as far as working out if there is a word for 'urgency' in Indonesian during my lessons, but a quick check on Google Translate as I type unsurprisingly reveals there isn't one. And that piece of linguistic knowledge is everything you need to know. Whether you're arranging meetings, expecting deliveries, need workmen or you're simply waiting for a beer, time has a different meaning to the one you're probably used to. Just embrace it—it can be frustrating but it can also remind you that the million miles an hour life you left behind isn't necessarily the right speed to be going.

Making It Happen

Gary Leighton owns several business in Bali, including Bali Expat Services (www.baliexpatservices.com) that specialises in visas and business set ups. Who better to ask for an overview of what it's like to run a business here?

What's it like to own and run a business in Bali? Firstly, when it comes to setting up, do your research. Find a reputable agent to take care of your affairs. I see many people asking questions on public forums to other expats and getting the wrong advice. It's great to get a feel and opinions from other expats but I wouldn't recommend getting legal advice from a Facebook page. Laws here can change regularly and without notice, so it's best speak to someone who deals with the laws every day.

Choosing your field is part of the challenge, which is true anywhere but especially in Bali. There are many restaurants, so if this is your choice you will need a point of difference. There's a high turnover here. The same applies if you choose villas and retail.

You don't need good staff; you need great staff. Bali is a very laid back place as we all know, but this can carry into the workplace, too. Don't get me wrong, I love the people here but some do need constant reminding and supervision. Don't expect the same amount of effort and diligence as you would from yourself. That can be true anywhere in the world, but especially here. I currently have great staff and the added bonus is that they are very nice people. They just sometimes need a nudge.

You will have to get used to waiting. Remember that nobody here is in a rush for anything unless it's the first of the month (payday). Be prepared for people to show up or deliver up to two hours late and think it's normal. Allow a big leeway of time in your diary if you're making appointments. Supply and service can be a guessing game and definitely keeps you on your toes.

With that in mind, if you don't have a lot of patience you will need to adapt very quickly. You sometimes have to learn to accept it is what it is; Bali is not going to change just because you can run a tight ship in your home town.

In saying all this I would still rather run a business here than in Australia. There's a lot less red tape, fewer regulations and a lot less stress. Once you have figured out that you can't change everything here and just roll with it, it's not a bad place to do business.

Management—Bali-style

CultureShock!'s Single White Female friend from Chapter Four, Kylie Turner, bagged a job here as a Brand Manager for Havaianas Indonesia back in 2013. This is her tale of managing a team in Bali.

When a much-coveted job in Bali is unexpectedly offered to you, with an all-expenses paid move from Australia, a great expat salary package and the promise of amazing weather, three-bedroom villa with a pool, sunsets and eternal cheap cocktails, do you really stop to consider if you're up for the challenge of actually getting work done in a Third World country? In my case, no.

After being briefed that my future General Manager (Indo-Chinese background, originally from Jakarta, worked in retail for over 15 years in Bali) was "not a very friendly person" (her own words to be fair), I took a risk, accepted the job and packed up my old life for this new one.

Indonesians can often be shy and awkward when encountering a new *bule* (as Westerners are affectionately called here), especially one in a senior management position, so walking into an office of 25 strangers and sitting at my desk was a little overwhelming for the first few weeks. Most of the staff avoided eye contact, then ogled when they thought I wouldn't notice. Once you form a bond or a shared joke, they let down the walls and are friendly and very sweet. There is definitely a 'people-pleasing' element to the culture where they are happy to help and so polite when they see you in need.

Being the only westerner with minimal local language often meant I missed the (apparently) hilarious things that happened. I developed serious FOMO (Fear of Missing Out) after the first few months and demanded to have all jokes explained to me once I felt comfortable in doing so.

Finding the right staff, with positive 'can-do' attitudes is imperative to your success in getting things done, as is knowing the strengths of your team members so as not to push them in areas they are not comfortable. Ensuring you have an excellent assistant or 'right-hand-man' who will understand you properly and explain to everyone else around you and help you translate your requirements is imperative.

That said, it's still challenging to get stuff done. It's almost always the opposite of what you ask for. You must check, check and check again. Then go direct to the supplier or factory before something is finalised and check it one last time. Chances are it will still somehow turn up wrong, so then factor in extra time to send it back and have it repainted, reprinted, or made from scratch.

The production levels and craftsmanship in Bali can be amazing and often with very affordable pricing, but attention-to-detail is not always a strong point. The easy going nature of Indonesians can often work against them.

An item produced from a clear and comprehensive brief will generally turn up in the wrong colour and size leading to the following type of exchange:

> Me: "Oh we requested this signage in red, remember?"

> Supplier: "Oh iyaaa, it's ok, this one white ya." (toothy grin and head nodding)

> Me: "Umm yes I can see its white, but no sorry Pak, we need it in red, it's the corporate colour" (also toothy trying-to-be-patient grin)

> Supplier: "Oh no problem, I think is OK. We leave in white ya? Same."

> Me: "Umm no, it's not the same, you are going to have to change it, ok, so when can you have it repainted in red?"

> Supplier: "Iyaaaa ok we do by this afternoon and bring to you." (realises smiling doesn't alleviate a pedantic expat who needs her job done so concedes to do it in half the time originally required)

When this newly painted red item is returned that same afternoon, the chances are the paint will still be wet and the delivery driver's fingermarks will be all over it. And so you smile and start again.

Doing business in Bali, the sooner you learn to breathe, and laugh (and factor in a three-week buffer period for any project), the sooner you will appreciate the carefree and whoopsie-daisy nature of the Balinese workers.

Be prepared to compromise, be late, miss deadlines, and try to adopt the same attitude—it will alleviate stress and stop you from losing your cool.

Conflict is almost never a way to get anything done here, the frozen faces and rigid expressions will teach you that the first time you raise your voice over something. This is not a successful way to communicate in Bali, and soon you will learn that your new best friends are patience and repetition… and repetition and repetition. Sorry, force of habit.

You will definitely work hard, get your hands dirty (literally; it's hard to NOT get your hands dirty in Bali. Carry hand sanitiser for when they are too dirty) but remember to smile and not take it all too seriously, and focus on sunset cocktails at the beach on Friday when the working week is over… or before Friday if it's all getting a bit too much.

Setting Up a Business

PT. PMA is the only legal form of company that a foreigner can own that allows them to run a business in Indonesia. Check the website www.baliexpatservices.com for setting up a business set up, although the requirements can change without notice.

These are the documents you should have to set up PT. PMA:

1. Proposed name of the company (three options)
2. Copy of ID for commissionaire and the director
3. Photograph
4. Copy of status of land or building certificate (Copy of the lease agreement)
5. Copy of land certificate
6. Copy of Land Tax Receipt (PBB)
7. Copy of building permit (IMB). Please note that the company can't be registered in a residential property.

These are the licenses that need to be processed:

- Initial Approval from Investment Coordinating Board
- Legalised name of the company
- Issued Article of Association by Indonesia Public Notary
- Local Authority permit Approval from Indonesia Village Chief and District Chief
- Tax Registration Code Number
- Legalised Company Article of Association from law department
- Location Permit and Nuisance from Regency
- Registration of Company Certificate from Trade and Industry Department
- Permanent Business License from Investment Coordinating Board)

VOLUNTARY SERVICE

So I've painted a picture of an idyllic paradise. Admittedly it's an honest picture—there's crime, there's frustrations, there's annoyances. Literally nowhere is perfect, but overall I evidently recommend my home as a great place to live. But while it's easy to enjoy Bali when you're a Westerner with a few quid in your pocket and Bali has undoubtedly benefited from the immense amount of foreign money flowing into it, not everyone benefits and while families usually look after their own that doesn't mean there aren't people who need help. So if you fancy doing some voluntary work in paradise there are plenty of opportunities. Whether you want to teach English, help out at a kindergarten, support children with disabilities or offer your time to the creatures of the world with a wildlife placement, there are plenty of opportunities. Check out www.gooverseas.com/volunteer-abroad/indonesia/bali for some good ideas.

Official Name
Bali—a province of the Republic of Indonesia

Capital
Denpasar. (The capital of Indonesia is Jakarta.)

Flag
The seal of Bali on an orange background. The seal is a blue pentagon with Balinese architecture and the legend 'Glorious Bali Island' on it. The Indonesian flag is much simpler, split horizontally in two halves with red on top and white below.

Time Difference
GMT +8. The capital of Indonesia, Jakarta, works on +7 and you may find certain businesses, especially banks, using this time.

Telephone Country Code
62

Climate
Bali has a tropical climate with two main seasons—wet and dry. The temperature remains stable throughout the year but the differing levels of humidity can mean it doesn't necessarily feel that way. Rainy season is from October to April with the worst rain from December to March (albeit the 2015-16 rainy

season didn't stick to those rules.) The central highlands tend to be cooler than the coast.

Population
4.225 million (as of 2014)

Language and dialect
The official language of Indonesia is Bahasa Indonesia. Balinese is the local dialect to Bali but English is widely spoken.

Religion
Bali is home to most of Indonesia's Hindu minority that accounts for the biggest proportion of the island's population. Over 80 per cent of the island's population is Hindu with approaching 15 per cent Muslim. Christianity and Buddhism make up the biggest share of the remainder.

Government type
People's Consultative Assembly of the Republic of Indonesia

Currency
Indonesian Rupiah

Industries
Tourism is the biggest industry on the island and is what accounts for Bali being one of Indonesia's wealthiest regions. Although tourism is responsible for the highest income, agriculture still employs the most people.

Exports
Arts, handicrafts and various crops.

Ethnic Group

The Balinese are an ethnic group native to Bali.

Airport

Girah Rai International Airport (Denpasar)

Electricity

Two-pin socket (22v / 50hz)

CULTURE QUIZ

QUESTION 1

The small baskets with offerings for the demons you see on the floor are called:

(a) *Segehans*
(b) *Canang sari*
(c) Basket cases

Answer: (a) *Segehans*. *Canang sari* is the name for the baskets that are put on the temples above ground for the gods while segehans are for the demons.

QUESTION 2

The Balinese wear belts when visiting a temple to:

a. Keep their trousers up
b. Make a fashion statement
c. Separate the pure and impure parts of their bodies

Answer: (c) The belts are a demarcation line for the different parts of the body

QUESTION 3

How do you say thank you in Indonesian and Balinese?

a. *Terima Kasih* and *Suksema*
b. *Terima Kasih* and Thanks
c. Cheers and *Suksema*

Answer (a). You can also shorten the Indonesian form to '*ma kasih*' and be understood.

QUESTION 4

When you drive a scooter around Bali you must have the following kind of licence?

(a)   International or Indonesian

(b)   That of your home country

(c)   Licence? Who cares? This is Bali

Answer: (a) And remember it's not just a legal requirement but almost certainly needed for your travel insurance too.

QUESTION 5

What is the name of most popular local beer?

(a)   Star

(b)   Bintang

(c)   BeerBali

Answer: (b) Bintang. Bintang means 'star' and you'll notice the label has one on it.

QUESTION 6

Why do Balinese only build one-storey houses?

(a)   Because they have a fear of stairs

(b)   So old people don't have to climb stairs

(c)   Because they don't like having feet above their heads

Answer: (c) Because they don't like having feet above their heads. Feet are impure, but the growing urbanisation has led to exceptions being made in cities.

QUESTION 7

Why does Bali's airport close down for a day once a year?

(a) To clean the sand off the runway

(b) For the annual Nyepi festival

(c) Because even planes deserve a day off

Answer: (b) For the Nyepi festival all travel, noise and movement is completely banned other than for emergency services. And flights are not an emergency service.

QUESTION 8

What does '*Saya bisa bicara bahasa* Indonesia' mean?

(a) I can speak Indonesian

(b) Are you a Martian?

(c) That sunset is lovely

Answer: (a) I can speak Indonesian. If you want to say you can't speak Indonesian, then put the word '*tidak*' (no) between '*Saya*' and '*bisa*'

QUESTION 9

Why is there an annual celebration on 17 August?

(a) It's Balinese flip-flop day

(b) Indonesian Independence Day

(c) To make offerings to the rice gods

Answer: (b) Indonesian Independence Day. Independence was declared on 17 August, 1945 but was not recognised by the Dutch until years later after an armed struggle.

QUESTION 10

What's the best thing about Bali?

(a)   The ricefields

(b)   The sunsets

(c)   The people

(d)   All of the above and more

Answer: (d) If anyone got that one wrong then I haven't done my job properly writing this book.

DO'S AND DON'TS

DO

- Say hello to everyone—it's an easy place to be approachable.
- Explore—there's much more to Bali than the tourist centres.
- Try the streetfood—There's more to Bali than high-class restaurants.
- Try surfing—If you don't try here, where will you?
- Island hop—Use Bali as a jumping off point for exploring Indonesia.
- Be polite—Take your shoes off when entering a Balinese house.
- Respect the religion—Wear a belt in a Balinese temple.
- Take care—Be aware of your surroundings when using ATMs
- Speak the language—Learn a few words of Bahasa Indonesia.
- Haggle—There's nothing like a good haggle, but don't go too far for the sake of a dollar.
- Watch a dance—It's the perfect example of Balinese culture.
- Watch the sunset—as often as you can. It never gets old.
- Use your horn when you drive a moped—It's a way of telling people you are there.

DON'T

- Drink the water from the tap—Bali belly ain't fun.
- Swim where the red flags are out—The rips are dangerous.
- Invite trouble—Put handbags over your head when on a scooter.
- Forget what you'd do at home—Wear a helmet on a moped.
- Touch someone's head—It's disrespectful.
- Enter a Balinese temple if you're female and it's that time of the month—sorry!
- Buy drugs—It's never worth the risk.
- Point with your index finger—It's rude, you know.

GLOSSARY

Please refer to Chapter Eight for more detailed information on the structure of the language and some basic phrases and pronunciation guides. But here's a list of words that should get you through the day.

GREETINGS

Halo	Hello
Selamat pagi	Good morning
Selamat siang	Good afternoon (11-3)
Selamat sore	Good afternoon (3-6)
Selamat malam	Good evening
Sampai jumpa	See you (Goodbye)
Sampai jumpa nanti	See you later (Goodbye)
Apa kabar	How are you?
Siapa nama kamu	What is your name?
Nama saya	My name is

BASICS

Ya	Yes
Tidak	No
Mungkin	Maybe
Terima Kasih	Thank you
Permisi	Excuse me
Silakhan	Please (NB—not used at the end of a request) You, them and I
Saya	I
Kamu	You

Kita	We
Mereka	They

BASIC VERBS

Siapa	Who
Boleh saya	May I
Bisa	Can
Mau	Want
Pergi	Go
Datang	Come
Makan	Eat
Minum	Drink
Apa	What
Ada	There is / I have / Do you have
Suka	Like (as in approve)

HANDY WORDS AND PHRASES

Ini	This
Itu	That
Bagus	Good
Baik	Good afternoon (3-6)
Sudah	Already
Tidak apa-apa	It's OK
Maaf	Sorry
Hati-hati	Be careful
Di mana	Where
Dari di mana	Where are you from?
Ingriss	England
Amerika	United States

Australia	Australia
Dari di mana	Where are you from?
Saya bisa bicara	I can speak
Saya tidak bisa bicara	I can't speak
Bahasa Indonesia	Indonesian
Jalan	Street / walk
Berapa	How much
Mahal sekali	Too expensive
Jam berapa	What time is it?
Taksi	Taxi
Sama meter	With meter (a request for taxi drivers)
Kiri	Left
Kanan	Right
Mungkin nanti	Maybe later
Lain kali	Another time

EATING OUT

Kopi	Coffee
Nasi	Rice
Nasi goreng	Fried rice
Nasi campur	Mixed rice
Sate	Satay
Garam	Salt
Gula	Sugar
Ayam	Chicken
Babi	Pork
Sapi	Cow

Udang	Shrimp
Satu lagi	One more
Besar	Big
Kecil	Small
Tidak panas	Not spicy
Panas	Hot
Dingin	Cold
Tanpa	Without

IN AN EMERGENCY

Rumah sakit	Hospital
Dokter	Doctor
Membantu	Help
Polisi	Police

RESOURCE GUIDE

NGURAH RAI INTERNATIONAL AIRPORT

Web: www.imigrasi.go.id/index.php/en/
Phone: +62 (0)361 751038
Address: Jl. Ngurah Rai Kuta
Email: kanim_denpasar@imigrasi.go.id

EMBASSIES

Most embassies are in the Indonesian capital of Jakarta, but Bali's popularity means that many western countries have consulates here. For the most up-to-date information, Google is your friend but here are the details for three of the largest.

Australian Consulate

Web: bali.indonesia.embassy.gov.au/
Phone: +62 (0)361 2000 100
Address: Jl. Tantular Renon No. 32 Denpasar
Email : bali.congen@dfat.gov.au

British Consulate

Web: www.gov.uk/government/world/organisations/british-consulate-bali
Phone +62 (0)21 2356 5200
Address: Jl. Tirta Nadi 2 No. 20, Sanur
Email Consulate.Bali@fco.gov.uk

US Consular Agency

Web: surabaya.usconsulate.gov/bali2.html
Phone: +62 (0)361 233 605 After Hours Emergencies: +62 (0)81 133 4183
Address: Jl. Hayam Wuruk 310, Denpasar
Email: BaliConsularAgency@state.gov

IMMIGRATION OFFICES
Central Office
Web: www.imigrasi.go.id/index.php/en/
Phone: +62 (0)361 227828
Address: Jl. D.I Pandjaitan Niti Mandala Renon, Denpasar
Email: kanim_ngurahrai@imigrasi.go.id

EMERGENCY NUMBERS
- Police   110
- Fire brigade   113
- Ambulance   118

Note: While the ambulance number is listed above, it is often just as simple to grab a taxi to take you where you want to go.

HOSPITALS
International SOS Bali Clinic
Web: www.sosindonesia.com
Phone: +62 (0)361 710505
Address: Jl. By Pass Ngurah Rai, Denpasar
BIMC Hospital—Kuta
Web: www.bimcbali.com
Phone: +62 (0)361 761263
Address: Jl. By Pass Ngurah Rai 100x, Kuta
BIMC Hospital—Nusa Dua
Web: www.bimcbali.com
Phone: +62 (0)361 3000 911
Address: Kawasan BTDC Blok D, Nusa Dua
Siloam Hospitals Bali
Web: www.siloamhospitals.com
Phone: +62 (0)361 779900
Address: Jl. Sunset 818

Kasih Ibu Hospital
Web: www.kasihibuhospital.com
Phone: +62 (0)361 223036
Address: Jl. Teuku Umar 120 Denpasar

Sanglah Hospital
Web: www.sanglahhospitalbali.com
Phone: +62 (0)361 2279 1115 / 225 482
Address: Jl. Diponegoro Denpasar Bali

Surya Husada Hospital
Web: www.suryahusadha.com
Phone: +62 (0)361 233787
Address: Jl. Serangan No.1-4, Kota Denpasar

Ubud Clinic
Web: www.ubudclinic.baliklik.com
Phone: +62 (0)361 974911
Address: Jl. Raya Campuhan 36 Ubud

POLICE STATIONS

Denpasar
Phone: +62 (0)361 225456
Address: Jl. A Yani, Denpasar

Badung
Phone: +62 (0)361 829924
Address: Jl. Kebo Iwa, Mengwi Badung

Sanur
Phone: +62 (0)361 288597
Address: Jl. By Pass Ngurah Rai, Sanur

Nusa Dua / Bualu
Phone: +62 (0)361 772110
Address: Jl. By Pass, Nusa Dua

Kuta
Phone: +62 (0)361 751598
Address: Jl. Raya Tuban, Kuta
Ubud
Phone: +62 (0)361 975316
Address: Jl. Raya Ubud

TAXIS
Blue Bird
Web: www.bluebirdgroup.com
Phone: +62 (0)361 70 1111
Address: Jl. Raya By Pass Nusa Dua No. 4, Jimbaran
Express Group
Web: www.expressgroup.co.id
Phone: +62 (0)361 777723
Address: Jl. By Pass Ngurahrai, No. 57 XX, Jimbaran

Note: Uber and GrabTaxi work in Bali but there is a real pushback against them by the local taxi drivers. Also consider Go-Jek—an app that allows you order moped taxis in the same way you would an Uber. Always ask taxi drivers to put their meter on before you get in the car and start your journey.

SCHOOLS
Canggu Community School
Web: www.ccsbali.com
Address: Jl. Subak Sari, Banjar Tegal Gundul, Canggu, Badung
Phone: +62 (0)361 8446391
Email: admissions@ccsbali.com

AIS Indonesia (Australian International School)

Web: www.ais-indonesia.com

Phone: +62 (0)361 734 936 / +62 (0)361 734 937

Address: Jl. Kerobokan Raya No. 44, Banjar Taman, Kuta

Email: bali@ais-indonesia.com

Montessori School Bali

Web: www.montessoribali.com

Phone: +62 (0)361 730 028

Addresses:

- Preschool
  Seminyak Campus
  Jl. Lasmana No 66X
  Oberoi, Kerobokan
- Primary and Adolescent Community
  Umalas Campus
  Jl. Bumbak Umalas
  Gg. Villa Onga, Kerobokan

Bali International School

Web: www.baliinternationalschool.com

Phone: +62 (0)361 288770

Address: Jl. Danau Buyan IV no 15, Sanur

Email: admissions@baliis.net

Green School Bali

Web: www.greenschool.org

Phone: +62 (0)361 469 875

Address: Banjar Saren, Jl. Raya Sibang Kaja, Abiansemal

Email: admissions@greenschool.org

LANGUAGE SCHOOLS

Cinta Bahasa

Web: cintabahasa.com

Phone: +62 (0)812 3916 5005

Address (main): Jl. Raya Sanggingan 88x, Ubud

Email: learn@cintabahasa.com

Seminyak Language School

Web: www.learnindonesianinbali.com

Phone: +62 (0)361 733 342

Address: Jl. Seminyak No. 7, Seminyak

Email: sls.bahasa@gmail.com

IALF

Web: www.ialf.edu

Phone: +62 (0)361 225 243

Address: Jl. Raya Sesetan 190, Denpasar

Email: ialfbali@ialf.edu

BOOKSHOPS

Periplus

Web: www.periplus.com

Address: Multiple locations

Gramedia

Web: www.gramedia.com

Address: Several locations

WHSmith

Web: www.facebook.com/WHSmithIndonesia/

Address: Several airport locations

MEDIA

In the digital age the lines between what defines a newspaper, a magazine and a website have become increasingly blurred. Print publications are increasingly evolving their digital presence and, like my own *Essential Bali*, some choose to go completely digital. And when you're on the move or planning something, websites and Facebook pages can be easier and certainly more contemporary. Here's a selection of offerings to get you started.

Essential Bali
Guide to hotels, restaurants, spas and what's happening in Bali.
Web: essential-bali.com

Bali Bible
Popular social media-inspired guide to all that's good in Bali
Web: www.thebalibible.com

Honeycombers Bali
Another guide to what's happening on the island
Web: thehoneycombers.com/bali/

Bali Advertiser
Free newspaper and accompanying website specialising in adverts for the expat community
Web: baliadvertiser.biz

The Bali Times
Island-specific newspaper with complementary website
Web: www.thebalitimes.com

Bali and Beyond
A high-end magazine covering the island and its neighbours
Web: baliandbeyond.co.id

The Yak

Glossy magazine covering fashion, culture and nightlife in Seminyak

Web: www.theyakmag.com

The Beat

What's on when in Bali in this listings guide

Web: beatmag.com/bali

Jakarta Post

Indonesian newspaper that includes the Bali Buzz with the latest in Bali news

Web:www.thejakartapost.com

Hello Bali

Print magazine found in hotels and restaurants with reviews and features

Web: hellobalimagazine.com

Now! Bali

Magazine covering the latest in news, cultural features and reviews

Web: nowbali.co.id

FURTHER READING

Bali Chronicles, Willard A. Hanna, Periplus: Singapore, 2004.
- Explores the interaction between Bali and the west and how those encounters have affected the history and culture of the island.

A Short History of Bali, Robert Pringle, Allen & Unwin: Australia, 2004.
- Does what it says on the tin, exploring the history of Bali from its early infighting to western influence and colonisation through to independence.

Hotel K: The Shocking Inside Story of Bali's Most Notorious Jail, Kathyrn Bonella, Pan MacMillan: Australia, 2011.

- Behind the scenes at the place you definitely don't want to stay when you're here. Kerobokan Jail, known as Hotel K, is not on Tripadvisor for a reason.

Snowing in Bali: The Incredible Inside Account of Bali's Hidden Drug World, Kathyrn Bonella, Pan MacMillan: Australia, 2012.

- Bonella tells a tale of drugs, corruption and greed that dominated Bali for some time and still has an influence now despite the potential punishments.

My Life in Bali, Sandrine Soimaud, PT CCI: Indonesia, 2007.

- This is a classic example of a book aimed at children that is equally as educating for adults. A succinct description of the island's culture and traditions.

Eat, Pray, Love, Elizabeth Gilbert, Riverhead Books: US, 2016.

- It's never been on my reading list but that one woman's search for everything and the subsequent film brought further exposure and fame to the island.

Bali: Heaven and Hell, Phil Jarratt, Hardie Grant: Australia, 2015.

- Phil has been in Bali nearly for several decades and he brings all his knowledge to bear in this tome exploring the modern culture and history of the island.

Bali: A Paradise Created, Adrian Vickers, Penguin / Tuttle: Australia, 1989.

- We know Bali is popular and I hope I have shed some light on why, but Vickers goes into much more detail to unearth its allure and development.

ABOUT THE AUTHOR

Paul Winslow is a travel junkie who left the UK to go travelling at the end of 2009 and never made it back. After a year on the road he 'settled' in Melbourne for over three years before washing up on the shores of Bali in 2014. He edits a digital guide to the island called *Essential Bali*—an excuse to stay at the best hotels, eat at the best restaurants and get pampered at the best spas. He also freelances as a journalist and communications specialist and since deciding to write this book also took on a role as a Marketing and Communications Manager.

He has an unhealthy love of cricket and combines that passion with travel to follow the England cricket team around the world, an addiction that led to the publication of his first book, *Going Barmy*. Paul lives alone in Bali; alone if you discount the lizards and mosquitoes that frequent his open living house. And the squirrels who steal his bananas.

INDEX

A

address 88, 173
Agung, Mount 18, 19, 20, 24, 35, 64, 134, 135, 149, 153, 162
airport 3, 7, 12, 75, 100, 127, 147, 163, 190, 203
alcohol 43, 58, 93, 108

B

Bahasa Indonesia 69, 165, 166, 169, 170, 186, 192, 196
Balinese dance 154, 155, 157, 158
Balinese food 114, 116, 117, 119
Balinese house 64, 192
Balinese people 5, 19, 42, 44, 50, 61, 63, 67, 78
banjar (neighbourhood watch) 54
banking 77, 85, 90
Batukaru, Mount 20
Batur, Mount 20, 133, 150
beach 7, 9, 12, 13, 28, 60, 61, 72, 113, 119, 125, 126, 127, 132, 136, 138, 139, 158, 162, 182, 210
Bintang 8
brunch 125, 126
buffalo racing 160
bule (foreigner) 60, 98, 173, 180
business *(see also* PT.PMA) 5, 11, 24, 29, 33, 37, 40, 59, 73, 74, 75, 84, 90, 112, 117, 129, 130, 175, 176, 177, 178, 179, 180, 181, 182

C

Canggu 17, 28, 103, 132, 137, 201
cash 13, 73, 77, 81, 83, 84, 108, 176
ceremonies 13, 14, 47, 48, 50, 54, 146, 163
climate 27, 28, 107, 185
coffee 8, 128, 129
community 48, 51, 58, 124, 128, 204
crime 55, 183

D

Denpasar 17, 34, 95, 153, 185, 187, 198, 199, 200, 203
Dhyana Pura 14
diving (scuba) 142, 143, 144
driving licence 95, 98, 99, 108
Dutch rule 33, 34

E

eating out 10, 58, 111, 124, 128, 132

F

family 13, 26, 44, 48, 49, 55, 56, 58, 61, 64, 103, 111, 114, 117, 163
festivals 162
football 60, 93, 136, 160
furniture 84, 85

G

gamelan 154, 155, 156
getting around 94
Gili Islands 143, 160, 161, 162
golf 116, 147

H

healthcare 105

I

insurance 79, 98, 105, 106, 189
Internet 86, 87

K

KITAS 73, 75, 77, 81, 82, 98
Kuta 14, 17, 28, 54, 93, 102, 113, 132, 135, 136, 138, 147, 148, 161, 162, 198, 199, 201, 202

L

language 9, 44, 67, 69, 105, 161, 165, 166, 167, 168, 173, 180, 186, 192, 194
Legian 6, 17, 28, 132, 136, 161
Lombok 16, 30, 33, 37, 39, 42, 160, 161, 162

M

Majapahit Empire 29, 30
massage 11, 142, 145, 146, 147
moped *(see also* scooters) 6, 8, 52, 75, 99
mountain biking 144
mountain climbing 149, 161

N

names 56, 86, 89, 122
nightclubs 136
Nusa Dua 13, 17, 132, 138, 147, 149, 199, 200, 201

O

owning property 91

P

pembantu (helper) 52, 87
phones 87
pronunciation 173, 194
PT.PMA *(see also* business*)* 177
puputan (mass suicide) 37

Q

quad biking and tubing 144

R

religion 29, 30, 33, 42, 44, 46, 48, 58,
  105, 153, 192
rent 14, 52, 82, 83, 84, 90, 95, 178
restaurant 24, 40, 45, 54, 111, 113,
  120, 121, 122, 123, 124, 128, 129,
  136, 158, 167, 176, 177, 178

S

Sanur 37, 103, 135, 137, 198, 200, 202
schools 103, 139, 143, 168
scooters *(see also* moped*)* 13, 55, 75,
  95, 99, 101, 102, 189, 193
seasons 27
segehans (offerings) 70, 188
Seminyak 6, 8, 10, 14, 17, 28, 54, 55,
  89, 101, 102, 121, 129, 132, 135,
  136, 137, 151, 158, 161, 202, 203,
  205
shopping 91, 93, 94, 100, 132, 136,
  143, 161
SIM cards 87
sockets 85
spas 145, 146, 147, 204, 209
supermarkets 10, 11, 91, 92, 93
surfing 93, 138, 139, 140, 141, 142,
  144, 192

T

Taman Nusa 157
Tanah Lot 14, 135, 147, 148, 150, 151,
  153
tax 81, 82
taxis 99, 201
temperature 27, 185
temples 14, 25, 45, 47, 49, 64, 65, 70,
  84, 85, 89, 116, 117, 135, 147, 151,
  152, 153, 157, 188, 192, 193
traffic 8, 9, 12, 13, 14, 36, 49, 54, 55,
  75, 86, 99, 101
trekking 135, 144, 161

U

Ubud 13, 17, 25, 103, 116, 122, 132,
  133, 137, 141, 142, 153, 157, 200,
  201, 203

V

visa 73, 74, 76, 81, 95, 98
voluntary work 183

W

warung (family restaurant) 26, 96, 111,
  113, 127, 138
white water rafting 137, 144
wildlife 25, 158, 183
wine 40, 55, 128
World War II 34, 38, 134

Y

yoga 132, 141, 142, 147

Titles in the **CultureShock!** series:

Argentina	Great Britain	Russia
Australia	Greece	San Francisco
Austria	Hawaii	Saudi Arabia
Bahrain	Hong Kong	Scotland
Beijing	Hungary	Sri Lanka
Belgium	India	Shanghai
Berlin	Ireland	Singapore
Bolivia	Italy	South Africa
Borneo	Jakarta	Spain
Bulgaria	Japan	Sri Lanka
Brazil	Korea	Sweden
Cambodia	Laos	Switzerland
Canada	London	Syria
Chicago	Malaysia	Taiwan
Chile	Mauritius	Thailand
China	Morocco	Tokyo
Costa Rica	Munich	Travel Safe
Cuba	Myanmar	Turkey
Czech Republic	Netherlands	United Arab Emirates
Denmark	New Zealand	USA
Ecuador	Norway	Vancouver
Egypt	Pakistan	Venezuela
Finland	Paris	
France	Philippines	
Germany	Portugal	

For more information about any of these titles, please contact any of our Marshall Cavendish offices around the world (listed on page ii) or visit our website at:

www.marshallcavendish.com/genref